HOW TO MAKE YOUR BUSINESS YOUR MINISTRY

HOW TO MAKE YOUR BUSINESS YOUR MINISTRY

RHONDA WARE WILLIAMS

VISION GUARD

Vision Guard Publishing

This is for My Wild Friends

Let me give a big shout out to my wild friends – not the ones who have it all together but the ones who know they sometimes need a little help.
This is for my wild friends.

Not the ones who think everyone else is the problem but the ones who know they have some responsibility for the way things are.
This is for my wild friends.

Not the ones who think that everything would be better if other people would act right, believe right and choose right but to the ones who, despite the differences, love anyway.
This is for my wild friends.

Not the people who seek to control others, not the ones who expect everyone else to change, not the ones who are content with mediocrity but the ones who refuse to let their wings hang low. Even if they hit a few bumps along the way.
This is for my wild friends.

My friends who don't know why they act the way they do sometimes, my friends who think they may have a problem, my friends who almost gave up, my friends who wonder if anyone cares, my friends who wonder if there is a real solution for their issues, my friends who think most people are a little crazy and, like me, wonder if they are a little crazy too.

This is for my wild friends.

My friends, who, despite their shortcomings and difficulties, are still reaching out, hoping to discover the answers to their tough questions. This is for my wild friends who look at the world around them and declare, "Yes, I am wild but that strengthens me. I won't give up; I won't let go until I finish what I came to do."

This is for you wild friend. Let's fly!

Contents

Preface xiii

1
UNLEASH YOUR WILD VISION 1

One
EMERGE - Embrace Your New Opportunity 2

Two
CHOOSE - It's One O'clock 11

Three
REACH - Optimize Your Creativity 17

2
UNLEASH YOUR WILD PASSION 29

Four
ALIGN - Connect Your Actions to Your Purpose 30

Five
ACTIVATE - Connect Your Purpose to Your Ministry 46

Six
Advance - Connect Your Ministry to Your Business 59

Seven
ANTICIPATE - Connect Your Marketplace Ministry
To Your Life   77

3
UNLEASH YOUR WILD CAPACITY   **91**

Eight
BUILD AND MULTIPLY - Manage Your Money and
Your Motives   92

Nine
PRESS AND MOVE - Finish What You Start   106

Ten
STAND - Position Yourself For Victory   118

Bible Verses for Business Owners   141
About The Author   144

Introduction

Welcome Wild Friends

"Let your light so shine before men, that they may see your good works and glorify your Father in Heaven."
(Matthew 5:16)

My wild friends, I wrote **How to Make Your Business Your Ministry – The New Marketplace Ministry** to inspire you. The idea of being a business owner who makes good money, loves Jesus and lets your life be an example to the world is wild! You are special. Most people get caught up in the intoxication of wealth but not my wild friends. For you, money is not enough. It's fun. It gives you choices but it doesn't fill you up. Following other people is not enough because there's more inside of you than they see and you can't ignore it just to chase the crowd. You are wild and that's how God created you!

We are the ones who love God but often feel we are from another planet. With a real desire to excel in business and a genuine desire to honor God, He cut us from a different pattern. Praise God! He is not a duplicator with His creations.

I will never forget the sight of the empty shelves at my local Walmart at the beginning of the 2020 Covid-19 pandemic. I stood watching in shock as people frantically grabbed the leftovers from the paper product isle. At first, it was scary. I had never seen a time when a threat was so significant that the entire country shut down. I went home and planted myself in front of the TV and listened to frantic reports of growing Covid-19 cases. The more I listened, the more alarming the reports became.

We needed food, toiletries and of course, we were down to our last two roles of toilet tissue. Just as I drifted into the media infused fear of the unknown, a friend called with a happy, unconcerned voice.

"Hey, what's up?"

"I'm watching the news and wondering how I'm going to find some things that we need. Are you short on items too?"

"No, we're good. I talked to a few of my friends who work in stores. They told me when they expect supplies and when they are stocking the shelves." She helped me figure out where to go to shop and the best time to arrive at the store. It was all about the strategy. After a few days, I had enough supplies for my family and enough to help others as well.

I watched frantic people and fearful reporting about how many people were out of toilet tissue. But this friend ignored the reports and got what she needed. Her experience was different from most people because she didn't connect with the crowd. Instead, she found her own solution. That's a wild one!

After several months, I started thinking, "I need to learn to live in a Covid threatened world." I cut my TV watching down to one news story per day. I put some safety protocols in place, got vaccinated, updated my Zoom account and transitioned my business from face-to-face to mostly virtual. Then, I started making plans to take advantage of the extra time at home. Covid -19 brought an initial halt to my daily routines but making the right adjustments created new opportunities that shifted my perspective in ways that I never imagined. By the end of the year, 2020 was one of my most productive years.

The Covid pandemic taught me we often find great opportunities in the middle of challenges. When everyone runs in one direction, look around and ask yourself, "Is this really the best way?" While some people were panicking in the stores, others had inside knowledge about the best place and time to go to the store. They walked right in and got what they needed. Yes, the news was alarming. Instead of getting caught up in the gloom on the TV, they managed their situation without fear and panic. They adjusted and discovered new opportunities to progress in the middle of the panic and stepped into 2021 in better shape than before Covid -19. This opportunity is not just for them, it's available for you too. All you need is a clear vision, the courage to see life a different way and the boldness to **GO FOR IT!** That is the same out-of-the-box thinking that every person in marketplace ministry must embrace.

Seizing your marketplace ministry opportunity requires you to see beyond what's in front of you. It means looking past what other people are doing and instead gazing into your own vision, purpose and possibilities. It means looking closely at not only how you conduct your business and ministry but *why* you work in your business and ministry. This need for vision and purpose echoes through business and ministry, becoming the foundation for every decision you make. This opportunity is so significant that it creates a need for a realignment of your business and ministry to make sure your actions are pointing to your goals. When correctly executed, the proper alignment opens doors to new avenues for success and personal fulfillment that overflows into every area of your life.

Throughout this book, I reference true stories that show how God moved me from a corporate, self-focused identity to market-place ministry. I went from a corporate executive to ministry and business. Everything you are about to read applies in all the places where you function. Even if the environment does not allow you to talk about the Bible, it's okay; just love and help other people live better. Let your life tell your story.

How to Make Your Business Your Ministry – The New Marketplace Ministry is not for everyone. But if you will be a little wild and step away from normal, you'll see the many ways God wants to use you. Your ministry and business will align with a noble purpose. Opportunities to share your faith and show God's love will find you as your actions speak louder than your words. I am so excited about my wild friends who let their light shine in dark places.

Let's do this together.

"Now to Him who is able to do exceedingly abundantly above all that we ask or think, according to the power that works in us." (Ephesians 3:20)

Preface

Your Great Opportunity

"The true measure of success does not lie in how you use your money to change your life, but how you use your influence to change the life of others."

How To Make Your Business Your Ministry - The New Marketplace Ministry invites you to find purpose in ministry and business. Covid -19 helped us see that work and ministry continue even when we cannot see each other face-to-face. We learned to use digital sources for work and worship. It awakened us to the truth that you don't have to be face-to-face to conduct effective business and ministry meetings. You also don't have to be in a church building (although church attendance is a tremendous benefit) to do your ministry. We learned ways to interact, celebrate and find comfort, even when we had to stay 6 feet apart. Social distancing revealed the truth that we do not confine ministry and business to buildings. They go where you go. This realization creates so many opportunities that we are still unfolding what it really means.

Wild friends, the key is not the building. The key is you! Yes, we need our time together in buildings but it doesn't stop there. It is so easy to find comfort in daily routines with the security of watching other people stand on the stage of life. That works for a season to learn and grow but eventually you must stand on the stage that God has given you. If you love God and have a business or career, you have a great opportunity right where you are to make business your ministry.

In marketplace ministry, you bridge the gap between the church and the business world. You present new and easy ways for people to experience God's love. You are not afraid to get in the trenches, make money and manage your resources in a way that honors God. Business executives already know that principles like integrity and diligence are important factors for business success. These biblical principles cross the line, blessing anyone willing to embrace the truth. Here are some statements from the American Express website about their mission, vision and values: We Do What's Right. We Care About People. We Respect Our Communities.

Now look at these Bible verses:

"Do nothing from rivalry or conceit, but in humility count others more significant than yourselves. Do not merely look out for your own personal interests, but also for the interests of others." (Philippians 2:3, 4)

"In all things showing yourself to be a pattern of good works; in doctrine showing integrity, reverence, incorruptibility." (Titus 2:7)

"Love your neighbor as yourself. No other commandment is greater than these." (Mark 12:32)

Yes, successful businesses use biblical principles (even when they do not care about biblical values) because biblical principles work in business, especially when your motives honor God.

In the past, marketplace ministry primarily operated by providing spiritual guidance and support to people in business but we considered them ministers, not businesspeople. Business and ministry were separate with different people and different agendas.

Not anymore!

In the new marketplace ministry, wild friends go beyond the old model. We refuse to be banned by invisible lines that try to govern how successful we can be in business. Did you sign a vow of poverty? No! Just because you love God doesn't mean you can't live well. That's right. Go ahead, make your profit *and* run your business. Be a major player in your career or business. Instead of compromising and surrendering to traditional, political, self-absorbed business tactics, seek a higher level of commitment to people and biblical integrity. Become an example of how to create an environment where business and ministry work together. Show people the lifestyle of a follower of Christ who is successful in business. Let them experience God at work.

Everywhere you find people, there is a great opportunity to show an authentic, God-centered lifestyle. If people cannot see you, talk to you and engage with you, how can you make a difference? How will they know what authentic Christianity looks like? Marketplace ministry takes you inside, behind the scenes, where you become the decision maker. It gives you a great opportunity to influence people and demonstrate God's love.

Before you go any further in this book, take a moment and tell yourself, "God cares about me. He gave me gifts and a desire to use them. He gave me purpose and the talent to conduct business successfully. It is my responsibility to give all that I have in the environment where my gifts flourish."

"And whatever you do, do it heartily, as to the Lord and not to men, knowing that from the Lord you will receive the reward of the inheritance; for you serve the Lord Christ." (Colossians 3:23-24)

An unwavering belief in work as ministry determines how you decide, how you make money and what you do with the money you make.

How to Make Your Business Your Ministry – The New Marketplace Ministry, is a companion to coach you to become an influencer in business. Your influence gives you the opportunity to show God's love by your actions, not just your words – to be seen and known in business and ministry.

1

UNLEASH YOUR WILD VISION

One

EMERGE - Embrace Your New Opportunity

"Don't let old familiar habits invade new opportunities."

In the Beginning

It started because I couldn't sleep. Night after night, my mind wondered with thoughts like, "I know there's more for me." Something was missing. It felt like there was a deeper part of me inside, hiding behind the person who was a mom, wife and grant writer for an inner-city youth ministry. The inside me had beliefs, talents and desires that the outside me ignored. I knew there was more but no matter how I tried, I couldn't get to the place where I needed to be.

As you read through these chapters, you will hear me say, "It's one o'clock." That's what I say to myself when I need to make a decision that is bigger than my emotions and beyond my comfort zone. It's a way of life that summons your wild side to take control and move your life forward. I didn't know how to access my wild side back then but now I know. I'll tell you more about "It's one o'clock" in Chapter 2.

One of those sleepless nights, about 3:00 am, I sat up in bed and put myself on trial. I needed answers.

"Why did you stop making money?"

"Was it necessary to ignore your ability to make money so you could answer a call of God to do ministry?

"Did God tell you to do that or did you assume it was the right thing to do?"

"Do I represent God well when I can't afford to give a child $200 to go to summer camp?"

"Does my lifestyle attract people to God and make them want to know more or does it send them in another direction?"

"Is there a way to answer my call to use my gifts of teaching, evangelism, discipleship and exhortation and use my business talents?"

Before that day, I was certain I was doing ministry the right way. I understand there are many good answers to these questions. We all need help sometimes. But that is not what I meant. I was thinking about me, a healthy young woman with the ability to do much better than I was doing. I quit my job, gave up a lucrative career and started working in ministry. That honors God, right? At first it felt good but after a few months my good feeling started fading fast because of my unmet financial needs. My tipping point happened during a meeting with the children in our ministry.

"We're so sorry but we can't take all of you to camp this summer. We just don't have the money."

I remember the announcement like it happened yesterday. Me, nestled against the wall of the gymnasium, wishing I could disappear. Children, standing around with blank faces, as if they had heard it all before. The only difference is that this time, the hurt and disappointment came from me and our ministry team, the place where they went to find hope.

I was a grant writer for an urban youth ministry. Our team secured the funds to help disadvantaged children go to summer camp. The grant proposals were well-written and we had good connections but despite our efforts, we didn't secure enough money. That meant we couldn't take everyone. I saw the faces of each child wondering, "Will I get to go or will I have to stay at home?" It was my job to secure the funds to get them all to summer camp. On that assignment, I failed. That day, I saw the face of disappointment on over fifty children. It was hard but that was not the reason I couldn't sleep. Why did I believe I needed to leave the job that could have provided money for the ministry? What was wrong with my decision? I needed an answer quick. That's why I couldn't sleep.

It was only three years prior that I managed a sales territory and enjoyed a lucrative salary, travel perks, a company car and a bonus. Back then, I had the money to be the donor writing the checks instead of the one asking for money. I could have sent everyone to camp. I was one of several friends who gave up corporate careers for full-time ministry. It was the price you paid to serve God, right? In my mind going into full-time ministry was the right choice. My friends and I celebrated each other for quitting jobs and having faith. It worked for some friends but my story was different. My husband and I cut expenses, lived in a small apartment, shared one car, and stopped unnecessary spending. No matter what we tried, it still was not enough. My questions remained, "If I know how to make money, why am I living like this? Who is benefiting from my lack?" Neither my business nor my ministry was getting the job done.

A few weeks later, before the final camp payment was due, we got a call. A donor heard about our situation, stepped in and paid the remaining balance. I was grateful for the money but nothing compared to the awakening that began. Working in ministry was great but a new ministry was emerging.

The Big Shift

My wild side jumped out of the box. I grabbed my business skills and talents from the shelf and started looking for ways to make more money. A big shift in how I viewed ministry interrupted the old way of doing ministry. I wasn't sure how my new ministry would look but it had to be better than what I was doing. God didn't give me gifts and talents to sit on a shelf. He wants it all!

In the Bible, when a shift happened, God redirected people and started a new way of living. When the plagues fell on Egypt, God shifted His people from slavery, freeing them to go possess their promised land (Exodus 7:14-11:30).

Esther experienced a shift when she became queen, allowing God to use her to save His people from destruction (Read the story in the book of Esther).

They sold Joseph into slavery creating a shift in his life. God made him an influential leader who preserved His people through a treacherous famine (Genesis 37-50).

In a similar way, the shift from ministry *or* business to ministry *and* business opens possibilities that give you more options to use all your gifts and talents. No longer do you have to choose one or the other. In marketplace ministry, your business is your ministry. When you walk into the building, your ministry begins. Your ministry goes where you go.

Think about the functions of a ministry. There are activities designed to draw people to Jesus Christ. We worship, pray, mentor, serve and disciple. A large, well-organized ministry also has human resources, payroll, administration and a host of functions that are very similar to a business.

How do you make your business your ministry?

You bring all your joy and love for God with you to work instead of leaving it at the door. You don't hide it under your desk or shove it away in place of business. Instead, you live your faith everyday so the world can see you loving God. You're not obnoxious or difficult. You just live and strive to be a highly functioning, encouraging, hard-working, dedicated, reliable, trust-worthy person who loves God and is not afraid to show it. Ministry and business come together every time you care for someone and share your faith at work. It comes together when you help people and care about their concerns. It comes together when you give, serve and encourage. The word "ministry" comes from the Greek word diakoneo, meaning "to serve." In the Bible, ministry means serving God and people, not just to help but to show them God's love in action. True ministry always has a hope of drawing people into their own walk with God (see Matthew 20:28; Mark 10:45; John 13:1-17). True ministry doesn't just happen in churches. It happens through you and goes where you go. For a follower of Christ, it is never "just business." God's plan is always in the mix. Yes, make your profit but do it in a manner that honors God.

Marketplace ministry makes you see business differently. When you create goals, you consider how God wants you to conduct your business, instead of being just profit driven. You look to God for creative business solutions and seek His plan for your success. People in marketplace ministry are leaders who adjust their plans to God's plan. You stretch yourself and look for opportunities to build and grow. You become more thoughtful, creative and careful because you want to honor God in your actions.

When you make your business your ministry here's what happens:

- You remove invisible crutches from other people and cultural norms.
- You expand your borders and set your wild side free. That means something about you and how your business operates will be different. The book on how to run a business won't do it for you. You will edit the book and make it your own.
- You become strategic in your business as you consider how your decisions influence others. Your new strategy will test old relationships and create new connections.

Best of all, marketplace ministry humbles you and draws you closer to God. He takes center stage in your business and your life.

I wish I could say that the change is easy but it's not. When you decide to do anything that honors God, you attract opposition. Things slow you down and it's not always a coincidence. Knowing what to do when you have opposition is just one step. Pressing forward and possessing what you know is another level.

Have you read the story of Joshua and the conquest of Canaan (the book of Joshua in the Bible)? It is one of my favorite Bible studies. In one lesson I teach, we notice God gave Joshua and his people the promised land but they still had to fight before they possessed it. There was opposition standing in the way of their own land. Why did they have to fight for what was already theirs? Possessing their land was just one part of God's plan. They also needed to develop the character to represent God in the land.

Marketplace ministry has challenges but it's worth the effort. Being different requires bravery. It requires sacrifice and focus to do something that other people haven't embraced. You need time to develop the character to not just start a business but to operate your business to represent God. The good news is that the reward for making your business your ministry far outweighs the sacrifice. After all, most people in the United States spend more hours at work than at home. In the USA, the average full-time employee spent 8.5 hours working every weekday (U. S. Bureau of Labor Statistics). Employees spent another 5.5 hours working on weekends and holidays. That means the dominate space in a weekday happens at work, preparing for work and going to work. This is too much time to leave God out. Yes, you have questions that need answers but don't wait. Start where you are and give yourself time to develop what you need to move your business forward as a ministry.

Why wait to reach someone for a few hours on Sunday when you have a smorgasbord of ministry opportunities Monday through Friday? If you are an influential leader at work, then multiply the opportunity. When you are serious about your faith, you can't lay it down because you have a career. You and your faith are a package deal. When you show up, the business side of you is present and the part that is committed to God is also in the room. Instead of hiding your faith, you live your faith openly for the world to see. Your business and ministry coexist so people see what an authentic relationship with Jesus Christ looks like. You invite God into your business and create an atmosphere that attracts people to a relationship with Him and a desire to study His Word. All of this happens during your business activities. You still work to make money, grow your business and enjoy the lifestyle that success brings. But that's not all you do. Your marketplace ministry compels you to excel at work. Go ahead, be the top salesperson and get your bonus. But also, be a peacemaker who cares about others. Be visible and look for opportunities to share your life and your faith.

When you emerge, you make a commitment to show your faith right where you are. You abandon routine business transactions that do not honor God. You put a microscope on all your business actions to honor God. If you have an activity that goes against a biblical standard, you walk away and find a better way to get the job done. When you emerge, you learn about your spiritual gifts and put them in action. You don't just follow the normal work protocol to be successful. With your gifts and your highly efficient work ethic, you open doors not only for you to emerge but for the power of God to emerge through you. But none of this can happen until you decide to be what God has called you to be. There's a statement you'll read about in the next chapter called, "It's one o'clock!" That means it's time to emerge and choose what you are going to be. The people who work around your business need you. They need your business to be a ministry.

Reflections for My Wild Friends

Build relationships on a deeper level that go beyond work. Get to know people personally. Learn about their family, what they care about and how they spend time away from work. Find out what keeps them up at night and be a genuine friend who listens. Commit to pray for your business associates and ask God to bless them, protect them and draw them close to Him.

Avoid allowing the workplace to set the standard of behavior for how you work and interact. Pay attention and carefully navigate your day to be sure you avoid any pitfalls that compromise your faith. Do not allow attachments that give an appearance that you agree with something that does not honor God. Carefully hold up your commitment to a biblical lifestyle and be an example for others to follow. Be vigilant and be careful.

Let your actions and convictions agree. Talking and planning is not enough. It's good that you are wild with your out-of-box thinking. God made you that way. Be what you believe. Live your life at work with such certainty that people know where you stand, even when you say nothing.

Two

CHOOSE - It's One O'clock

"Some events are not worth your tears."

Before I met my husband, I was in a relationship with a man I agreed to marry. Everything seemed normal except for a nagging feeling inside that told me something was wrong; I tried to ignore it. I thought maybe shopping for a wedding dress would help but it just got worse. No matter how hard I tried, the feeling would not go away. Still, I kept planning to move forward. One night, the feeling that something was wrong overcame me. It was so strong that I checked with my family to see if everyone was alright. There was an urgency about the night that I could not shake. After a time of prayer, I realized that the feeling had something to do with the man I was dating. Every night, I prayed for God to reveal to me why I felt so uncomfortable about the idea of marrying the young man. I remember praying a wild prayer that went something like, "God, if

I cannot see what you are trying to tell me, do whatever it takes for me to get the message." I call it the "Mack Truck" prayer.

Finally, I couldn't take it any longer. In the middle of the night, I got out of bed, grabbed my keys, then drove 30 minutes to his apartment. As I approached the door, I heard a noise inside that sounded like a fire alarm. I knocked on the door at 3:00 am. For a moment, I stood at the door telling myself to go home. Don't be one of those girls who is so insecure you go knocking on your boyfriend's door in the middle of the night. But there I was, knocking and trying to convince myself that all was well. Deep inside, I knew it was where I needed to be. The loud horn of the fire alarm continued and suddenly the door sprang opened. There he was, shocked to see me instead of the apartment manager to fix the broken fire alarm. While there was no real fire, I was burning with anger when I looked behind him. There stood his ex-girlfriend, or perhaps current girlfriend. At that point, it didn't matter. It was over.

"God, how could you allow this to happen?" I yelled, laying in my bed of tears. "How many times did I pray and asked you if this was right? Why did you let this happen? Why God, why?" After about 30 minutes of frantically yelling at God, something strange happened. Impressed upon my mind were the words, "I didn't do this. You did."

Let's be clear, those were not my own words. I was too busy blaming God for what happened. I didn't have the maturity to take responsibility for my actions. While I was blaming God and languishing in my emotions, God was speaking, helping me realize He didn't create my situation. I did.

With tears rolling down my face and overcome with emotion, something happened. A ray of clarity beamed into my mind. In the middle of my emotional disaster, intense clarity flowed through my mind. With my eyes swollen red from crying, I started feeling grateful. Have you ever felt two opposing emotions at the same time? It can happen. I was sad and hurt, yet I was grateful that I finally got my answer. Through prayer, God led me to the truth. The man I was about to marry had issues and was not ready for a wife. You know if a person cheats during the engagement, it's highly likely it will happen in the marriage. If that night didn't happen, I would have entered a difficult marriage that may have ended in divorce. There are many divorced people who would easily trade my experience for the anguish of recovering from a broken marriage. Thank God I made a choice to go find the truth. I accepted the temporary tears as a welcomed trade-off for the heartache of a painful marriage.

Four hours later, I was still in my bed; the lies were still unfolding and the tears were still flowing. In another moment of clarity, I looked through my tears at the clock next to my bed. It was 8:00 am. I said to myself, "You have until one o'clock pm to get out of the bed and pull yourself together. Yes, it hurts but the person you're crying over does not deserve your tears." The words started giving me my power back. They didn't stop the pain but they got my attention and helped me focus. Now, the goal was to stop crying. I kept repeating those words in my mind, "He is not worth your tears. He is not worth your tears." It was working. The crying stopped.

Then the clarity quickly faded as new thoughts flooded my mind.

"I need to call everyone and tell them the wedding is off."

I looked at the clock again. It was 11:00 am. A little clarity came back but I pushed it away and rolled over crying again.

"How could I have ignored so many warning signs? How long had this relationship with his ex been happening? Was it the first time? Probably not."

I looked at the clock. It was 12:45 pm. I took a deep breath and clarity flooded my mind. I made a mental note that I only had 15 minutes left to stay in the bed wallowing in my hurt.

"I wonder who knew this was happening?"

I rolled over and looked at the clock; it was 1:00 pm. That's when I got up, took a shower and got dressed. I put on full make-up, styled my hair and moved forward with my life. I went to visit my mother and hung out with some friends. We laughed and made jokes about weddings and relationships. The hurt wasn't gone but at 1:00 pm the decision to carry on with my life brought new strength and determination. That night I laid down and slept well.

Two months later, I saw the young man and the feelings were gone! I was grateful that God saved me from a terrible decision. I was glad to be single and free. My friends laugh. "Maybe you were not that attached to the guy. No one gets over a person so quickly." I even laughed at myself.

Why Does This Decision Matter in Marketplace Ministry?

Embracing a commitment to follow biblical principles at work will require that you sometimes override your emotions to make the best decision. Just because you feel it, doesn't mean you should do it. It's one o'clock decisions take boldness, out-of-the-box thinking and the willingness to do things that other people are not doing. Your decisions will stand in the face of pain, questions, mistreatment, betrayal and hard work. When you commit to marketplace ministry, you eventually must make a decision that requires you to get up and move forward with the it's one o'clock mindset.

When it's one o'clock in your life, you make the God-honoring decision, even when you don't feel like it. This doesn't mean you don't have feelings or a desire for something different. It means you trust God and choose the greater good. We root this way of thinking in strength beyond emotions, vision beyond what we naturally see and faith that God has something better for us. This is a choice that happens without a grudge, manipulation or expectation from others. This decision requires a willingness to leave something behind, change something you once believed or do something that you never thought you would. It denies a victim mentality and does not seek sympathy from others. It is a bold statement that promotes care and unwavering dedication to do what is right, no matter the cost.

Making a tough decision empowers you. You realize that you have more choices than you thought. You also find new opportunities and increased expectations as you stand firm in your God-given strength.

I have shared this opportunity with many friends and family who stepped up and made the tough decision. As I stated earlier, it's one o'clock is not for everyone, it's a choice. However, if you plan to be effective in your marketplace ministry, serve God and fulfill the call on your life, at some point, you'll make a tough decision. There will be a time when the only route to the place where God is calling is through a tough decision. When something stands between you and the path that God has planned for you, you may have to say, "It's one o'clock."

You get a certain number of heartbeats to accomplish what God is calling you to do. If God is calling you to a deeper purpose in your career, you can't wait any longer. Now is the time to show strength beyond emotions and make some big decisions. God doesn't share the stage. It can't be all about you and all about God, too. You will see one key choice embedded in most tough decisions. At the core, a tough decision often requires you to make a choice that aligns your life with God's will and His Word.

I could forgive the young man for cheating but he was not free to enjoy a relationship with me again. I realized the value of what I offered in a relationship and the importance of having a man who understood how to treat a treasure. A few years later, I met my husband. We have been married for 25 years and have 2 lovely children. I am so glad I choose to make the big decision. I am so glad it was one o'clock.

Reflections for My Wild Friends

Pay attention to the still, small voice inside of you and connect to how God is leading you. Study the marketplace ministry Bible verses in the back of this book and look for ways to connect your personal situation with the scriptures. It's one o'clock started because something did not feel right. Before you decide on your marketplace ministry details, make sure you connect to God's plan, not just what He wants you to do but *how* He wants it done.

In marketplace ministry, there are many voices. You have the corporate culture, vendors, the people you serve, your career growth, money, spiritual commitments and God's Word for guidance. It is impossible to discern which voice is accurate without concentration, meditation on the scriptures and prayer. Listen carefully to how God is leading you. In marketplace ministry, we make decisions that are not always popular. We carefully consider new business opportunities and don't assume every money-making offer is right for us. Careful thought happens before we make alliances and agreements. We understand God can prosper us without us compromising. We remember the reason we do what we do is to honor Jesus first. Everything else stands behind Him.

Three

REACH - Optimize Your Creativity

"New experiences deserve fresh expectations."

"And from the days of John the Baptist until now the kingdom of heaven suffers violence, and the violent take it by force." (Matthew 11:12)

I read this verse for over twenty years and never really understood what it meant until now. I have heard one person teach on it and even she said there was more to understand. Most people who try to explain the verse are reluctant to embrace what the verse is saying but the passage is clear. Let's inspect the word "violence." It comes from the Greek word "biazetai" and means to force your way, press into or snatch. Also, notice "kingdom" of heaven is not the heaven that we think of when people pass away. That heaven does not suffer violence. This refers to an opportunity we have now. It's a way of experiencing life, acknowledging God as King of Kings and Lord of Lords (Rev 17:14). It is living in His divine order on earth. When you are committed to living according to God's principles and putting Him first, you will encounter a "force" that will try everything to stop you. It will press you and try to snatch you away from your goals and away from God.

In ministry, when you are "all in" you'll see things happen that try to snatch you away. You must press in with all that you have and persevere through doubt and hinderances. Get comfortable being different. Let God lead you to experience how He does things. God has ideas and concepts that other people have not imagined and He will share them with people who follow Him. He is the greatest creator that we will ever know. He makes something out of nothing, simply by speaking. His creations have beauty in the smallest places and in large places; He cares about every detail. What's amazing is that He gave many of you a talent of creativity. Now it's time to press the boundaries and take your creativity to new levels through your marketplace ministry.

In the beginning, God created... Yes! He made something from nothing. (Genesis 1:1).

Creativity in Marketplace Ministry

Creativity is a gift. We see it used in the music industry, theater, art and many other facets of life. It's easy to see creativity in these normal spaces but there is so much more that we don't see, like opportunities for you to make a difference for yourself and others.

The gift of creativity is unmatched. It brings to life the secrets of the heart while prancing on the fingertips of emotions and feelings. Creativity opens doors that the troubles of life would otherwise lock. Do you want to step into corridors that are locked away from normal, everyday life? If so, be creative.

Creativity is the catalyst that makes memorable experiences that attract and keep people but before you flow in your creativity, you'll have to flow in your freedom. Why? Because the foundation of creativity is the freedom to be different and do something in a way that no one else is doing. It takes courage to be different and boldness to believe your different approach is good, maybe even great.

Finding a new level of creativity for your marketplace ministry is possible but you must press deeper to discover it. God does not give gifts just for you to enjoy. He gives them for the betterment of other people to be used to the fullest degree. Praise God for everything He gives you.

If you find it difficult to stir up your creativity, work with a person who is naturally creative. Look for someone who is not in your normal circles to give you a fresh perspective. When you work as a team, finding a new level of creativity becomes faster and more productive.

Why is creativity so important in ministry and business? Because creativity attracts people. It draws people emotionally and physically. It stirs the senses; makes you feel, laugh, think and desire. God, the master creator, gave us colors, aromas and beauty from the depths of the ocean to infinite heights in the sky. There are no limits to His creative ability and He shared this beautiful attribute with you and me!

"For by Him all things were created, both in the heavens and on earth, visible and invisible, whether thrones or dominions or rulers or authorities —all things have been created through Him and for Him." (Colossians 1:16)

Think of the organizations that you appreciate most. Browse through their websites and social media pages. Look for ways they use creativity to communicate and share their message.

See something you like? Why did it draw your interest? Did you click on anything? What made you click?

The need to be creative, different and fresh never ends. How you package your message should change to meet the communication styles of the culture and your desired audience and demographics. For example, there are many ways to get to a clear presentation of the gospel. Years ago, I learned what's called the Romans Road to Salvation. It's a great way to share your faith but it is not the only way. I know a man who said he embraced Jesus Christ while sitting at a bar as an alcoholic. Another alcoholic shared the gospel over beers, leading my friend to follow Jesus Christ. Another person I know said he was high on marijuana when he came across a Christian TV station and heard the gospel. As the speaker shared the gospel, the effect of the marijuana wore off. After years, he is still solid in his faith. As wild as it seems, God is very creative with how He communicates with us. Nothing stops Him. Being creative in your business and ministry is crucial to avoid falling short of the results that are available to you.

It's time to stop looking at what others are doing and ask God to show you what He has for you.

Are you being creative as you expand your marketplace ministry? Spend some time in prayer and ask God for new ideas and concepts. Don't simply look at what other people are doing. Be open to new ways that God has just for you.

Here are a few examples:

- Write a book that helps people and connects to your marketplace ministry goals.
- Host an event that attracts your target audience.
- Start something new that you have not done before.
- Do something fun to meet the people in your community.
- Create a theme that connects to your marketplace ministry.
- Develop an online persona that connects with your business and marketplace ministry.

- Add something special to every meeting (games, music, jokes or a new dish).
- Add a theme to your office, products, website and social media sites.
- Do something that no one else is doing in your industry.

Once you decide what to do, dig deep into your creative resources to figure out how to get it done.

Are you ready to create something amazing for your ministry and business?

Start with prayer. Talk to God about what you want to do and what He wants to do through you. Be willing to consider things that you have never done before. Be open and start asking questions like, "What do people want to feel when they work with me?" How should your ministry make them feel? When they experience your ministry, what should they see and what should they hear? How will you offer an uncommon experience?

Now, make a list of ways to answer the questions. Find a quiet place where you can think. Get with your team (or friends) and streamline your list until you find the right creative direction. After you have enough ideas, lay the list aside for a few days and come back to see which ideas are best. Then consider other needs like money, space, people, marketing, supplies, etc.

Keep praying and keep making updates and changes as needed. If your creative direction is working, continue to move in that direction. If something is not working, don't be emotional about it. Stop, regroup and try again.

Even if you find a successful creative path, it will continue to change. Continue to make changes, stay relevant, be exciting and keep growing.

God has enough creativity for everyone. All you have to do is tap into the gift, be flexible and let the creativity flow.

Let's look closer at how to add creativity to your specific marketplace ministry. Here are some situations where I have assisted business owners.

Case #1 - A Restaurant Business or Food Truck

A young couple planned to open a street café to sell flavorful burgers and sides from their food truck. The husband was a skilled cook and loved for people to enjoy his delicious food. However, he and his wife also felt called to ministry and wanted to create opportunities to share their faith and encourage people to hang in there when things got tough. With a little coaching, here are the ideas that surfaced.

- Place decorative, inspirational signs around the eating area.
- Host a regular outdoor Bible study around their food truck.
- Host outdoor worship events featuring local artists and nearby churches.
- Create an encouraging statement as a tagline for the business (not just about food but speak to the heart).
- Create some specialty items on the menu and give them encouraging names (sunshine plate, joy sauce).
- Develop a brand of excellent service and care for every customer. Be a friend and a listener.
- Create a website with posts that connect food to joy, community and family.
- Encourage membership and create some activities and benefits that make membership valuable.
- Support a local organization and become known in the community.

Case #2 - An Insurance and Financial Planning Agency

A woman who is a professional insurance and financial planner struggled with her commitment to ministry and her need to earn income. In the past, she worked fulltime in her business and spent several evenings and weekends doing her ministry. She was exhausted and always felt emotionally split between her two commitments.

With a little coaching, she reinvented her business as a marketplace ministry. We considered her spiritual gifts and looked for ways to incorporate those gifts into her daily business structure.

Here is what she did.

- She saw herself as serving her clients instead of as a salesperson.
- Her service meant she always looked for what was best for the customer, even if it meant a lower commission.
- She implemented 8 Principles of Marketplace Ministry (Ministryinbusiness.com).
- In her approach to business, instead of going for the sale, she got to know each person. She looked for ways to encourage people to make meeting her become a more memorable experience.
- She created content on her website to teach her clients about living a fulfilled life so they would enjoy their retirement.
- She prayed with customers and made phone calls just to check on them.
- She led an online Bible study and invited her clients and others to join her.
- On her website, she created content to make life better for the people she met.

Case #3 - A Motivational Speaker

A young man enjoyed a lucrative career as a motivational speaker. He held several contracts with Fortune 500 companies to deliver messages and courses to help with retention and employee satisfaction. Although his messages were inspirational, he desired more satisfaction with his work. He felt like he left his spiritual gifts on the table in pursuit of his speaking career.

After some discussions, he made a few changes. Here's what he did to create a marketplace ministry within his career.

- He primarily worked with corporations that did not want any reference to the Bible. However, he learned that people were receptive to a proverb, especially when he used it in a non-threatening manner. So, he added at least one proverb to every message.
- He started hanging around after his messages. Being available gave him an opportunity to engage in private conversations. He looked for ways to share his personal story and mention his faith. Sometimes people invited him to share more details and the door opened for marketplace ministry.
- When he traveled, he prayed for God to bring a person across his path who gave him a ministry opportunity. This is the part that amazed him the most because God answered this prayer! He has shared God's word on airplanes, hotel lobbies and even at a bar.
- He learned a few Bible verses, because he is usually not in a place to pull out a Bible, even on his phone. When the opportunity presented itself in private conversation, he often used the phrase, "Have you heard of that Bible verse that says...?"
- Before leaving home, he prayed for everyone on his schedule that day. The prayer was not just for a pleasant experience during the meeting. It was also for their business success, health, relationships and overall wellbeing. He always asked

God to bring peace and love to the person's life. He believed his prayers for others were the key to his own success.

After he became intentional about bringing his ministry to his business, he found business opportunities regularly during his travels.

Case #4 - A Personal Trainer and Nutritionist

A personal trainer and nutritionist loved helping people get in shape but also wanted to share biblical truths to help her clients manage their challenging issues. Although she struggled with sharing her faith freely, she found three Bible verses helpful.

- *Colossians 3:23* –"*And whatever you do, do it heartily, as to the Lord and not to men."*
- *Ephesians 4:29* –"*Let no corrupt work proceed out of your mouth, but what is good for necessary edification, that it may impart grace to the hearers."*
- *Matthew 5:16* –"*Let your light so shine before men, that they may see your good works and glorify your Father in heaven."*

The personal trainer made the following adjustments to change her business to a marketplace ministry.

- She realized she needed to remember the value of her work. She wasn't just helping people transform on the outside but was helping them on the inside too. In accordance with Scripture, Colossians 3:2, she began to work as if God was her boss. As a result, her clients had a more healing experience.
- She decided not to take part in any negative or condescending conversation (Ephesians 4:29). She found that taking part in

the negative conversation, even if it was true, made it difficult for her to see the best in her clients.

- She studied the fruit of the Spirit (Galatians 5:22-23) and let
  her fruit show everyday (love, joy, peace, patience, kindness,
  goodness, faithfulness, gentleness, and self-control).
- She lived out her faith openly so her clients could see it and
  feel it. She wanted them to feel the love and peace with every
  meeting.
- She handled every challenge by filtering her responses
  through the nine fruits of the Spirit.
- She used her spiritual gifts in every area of her business. She
  began to see better strategies for helping people feel better.
  Her students felt her patience and became less frustrated and
  more patient with themselves.
- She challenged her clients but also praised them for their
  hard work.
- Occasionally, a client felt comfortable enough to ask about
  how she stays so happy and positive. That's when the door
  opened wide for her to share how her faith guided her life.
  She saw herself as a link in the chain that helped people find
  joy in a relationship with Jesus Christ.

Marketplace ministry is not a typical business experience. It is
intentionally planned experiences that happen in unexpected places.
It happens right where you work and hang out. No matter where
you work or what business you own, there are a few points that
apply in every situation.

Your influence is crucial. Being a good influencer works better
when you are good at your job, a team player and easy to get along
with. It's hard for a person to listen to you share your faith when
they don't respect your work or behavior. That's why you must be

selective about the battles that you join. Always ask, "Who will my position offend? Is it worth it?"

In marketplace ministry, your love for God and His people is always on display. What you say and do matters. Leave an open door for anyone to look to you to share the good news of the gospel anytime and anyplace.

"Preach the word; be ready in season and out of season; reprove, rebuke, exhort, with great patience and instruction." (2 Timothy 4:2)

Reflections for My Wild Friends

God is the Master Creator. Instead of watching what other people do, spend time in prayer asking God for new ideas and concepts. As a follower of Christ, you have access to His rich storage of creative ideas for your business and ministry. Be willing to step out of the box and freely engage your creativity and see what God will do through you.

2

UNLEASH YOUR WILD PASSION

Four

ALIGN - Connect Your Actions to Your Purpose

"A God-ordained destination is always bigger than you."

As I walked up to a large, beautiful custom home, I noticed a young lady parked in front. Her car was a small SUV with signs glued on window and doors and covering the entire car.

"Don't buy this house."

"Don't trust this builder."

"Your house will fall apart."

I was just there to see the decoration but I couldn't help but ask, "What happened?" She was happy to share her story.

"They build big pretty houses with a poor foundation. My new home that they built cracked right down the middle. I am not the only person having problems with this builder. Look at these news stories."

She pulled out a large board with news articles glued from top to bottom.

"When you ask them to fix their mess, they ignore you."

"Wow, I am so sorry this happened to you."

"They are currently being sued but I just want my money back. I am not working and I will stand out here every day until they make this right."

The realtor in the house saw me talking to her and stood at the door, obviously trying to get me away from the girl and into the house. I walked in but thoughts of the distraught young lady parked outside overshadowed the joy of touring the big, beautiful home. I looked at the landscaped pool, outdoor kitchen, media room and the game room. However, all the beauty in the home meant nothing if the foundation was bad.

Later, I checked to confirm what the lady told me. An online search yielded story after story of complaints about the builder. There was even a story about the lady parked outside. That lady spent months during her unemployment, bringing terrible publicity to the builder. According to the online story, it was working. She spent all day going from one model home to the next, telling her story and people like me were listening.

Why is this important for marketplace ministry? Because the foundation that you build upon will determine the trajectory of your organization. No secrets. No short cuts. Take your time and pay the price to build well. It is important to build in a way that demonstrates a call of God on your life. Build right when people are watching. Build right when no one is looking. The goal is to build in a way that creates a legacy, not a temporary fix. Build as if God is in the room.

The foundational principles that you set in the beginning will live in people and their generations beyond your lifetime. How you talk to people matters. Your integrity, even in the trivial things, matters. What you post on social media matters. Your ministry page, business sites and yes, even your personal accounts matter. Integrity calls for you to be one person who is the same on all platforms. Yes, we are discreet in certain matters and we adjust our words for different places and people; yet there should never be a question about where you stand with biblical matters. The freedom of discretion must not conflict with biblical convictions. In marketplace ministry, your actions show your genuine care for the wellbeing of people, even when no one is watching. You never know when what you do will influence someone's decision or even their life. This requires intentionality and focus. It identifies you as a legacy leader, not just looking at what is happening now but making decisions that influence generations to come.

That home builder cut corners and used inferior products in building some of their homes. I'm sure they did not know that one angry girl who was out of work could damage their reputation and cost them sales and profits. They advertise as a builder of quality homes. But their actions told a different story.

When you're older, if you look back, you won't look at houses, cars and other material items to determine how good your life has been. You will look at legacy, the people who mattered and the time you spent together. You will think about who made a difference in your life and the people you helped. Questions will sift through your mind like, what did you leave that makes other people's life better? What did you do that will continue when you are gone? Did you honor God? Were lives changed because of you? How you answer these questions determines the extent of your legacy leadership.

Legacy Leaders

Legacy Leaders are people who advance by building a multi-generation marketplace ministry. This broad perspective on legacy drives the way you decide what to do and not to do. It helps determine what matters and what you don't have time for. It helps you connect your actions to your purpose. A Legacy Leader will say, "No," to most random offers that require time with no connection to purpose or priorities. Legacy Leaders understand that time is valuable.

They focus on five core values:

Longevity

Legacy Leaders see the big picture and stay the course through great adversity and change. When others give up, they continue. They stand firm in their faith, not relying on the culture to dictate their beliefs and convictions but adhering to the Scriptures, even when it is not a popular stance. They don't place deadlines on God. When they believe God is leading them in a certain direction, they stay the course until God says stop, change or move. They are in it for a lifetime!'

A clearly defined identity

Legacy Leaders understand who they are and what they bring to the table. They understand what God is calling them to accomplish and don't hide their gifts and talents but they continue to grow and expand them.

Exceptional leadership

Legacy Leaders are extraordinary leaders who masterfully and sacrificially guide their ministry and business. They lead creatively and boldly through personal loss, financial difficulty, emotional challenges and unmeasurable attacks. They lead through change, catastrophe, disappointment and failure. Leadership is a part of their identity and it shows up in every area of their business, ministry and personal life.

Authentic compassion

Legacy Leaders have a genuine care for the well-being of others. They believe they are called to make a difference in the lives of others. A Legacy Leader helps people find their way when they get lost in life's problems. They are forgiving and graceful. A Legacy Leader looks at the heart and believes in people's potential no matter what they have done. They are loyal and make great friends because of their level of compassion.

Unrelenting determination to follow God and His plan

Legacy Leaders have clearly defined goals and they stay true to their commitments. That means they keep following God even when they don't get what they want. When God leads, they stand firm, even when they don't see the full picture. When others turn around, they keep going, standing firm, even through tears and heartbreak. They abandoned all roads that go backwards. They trust God because He is God; He is good and He is sovereign. Legacy Leaders understand that some questions get answered in heaven but not on earth. They genuinely serve God with their whole heart even if they must wait until He gives them understanding.

Marketplace ministry is an excellent platform for Legacy Leaders because it expands their influence, creating a greater opportunity for multiplication. To maximize their platform, they need people and people need them. A follower of Christ who is successful in business, in culture and lives well without compromising faith is a significant benefit because they attract people. Yes! Be a strong Legacy Leader but also be a powerful business leader. How? By understanding the many ways to align your business and your ministry to advance in both arenas.

A business owner has responsibilities and goals, which include profits, shareholders, office management, service and human resource obligations. In business, a select group of executives who have different responsibilities and privileges make major decisions. A business environment also has unwritten rules that everyone knows to follow; we call it politics. In contrast, a marketplace ministry evens the field by valuing everyone and seeing people the way God sees them. Employees and customers get to experience authentic care in a business environment. Instead of business politics, you have business values that are based on the Scriptures. Everyone is equal. Everyone has value.

In the past, marketplace ministries operated as followers of Christ who served businesses. They enjoyed a great opportunity to provide spiritual guidance and support to people in business. The new marketplace ministry model goes beyond the old model and makes your business and your ministry coexist. That's right; advance, make your profit *and* have your ministry. Be a major player in the business world *and* serve God faithfully in ministry. However, instead of compromising and surrendering to traditional business politics, seek a higher level of commitment to people, biblical integrity and Legacy Leadership. Don't give up your biblical lifestyle because "It's just business." Create an environment where your money works for your ministry. Let them both honor God.

In most cases, it takes money to advance your business and ministry. That's why I am amazed when I encounter people in the Christian community who pretend money is not a big deal. It is a mode of exchange in the natural world. Your marketplace ministry needs income for certain operations and you need income for your own needs. I discuss money in "Chapter 8: Build and Multiply–

Manage Your Money and Your Motives." Yes, God cares about your money, and your motives but that's not all He cares about.

He cares about how you handle money (Psalm 37:21).
He cares about how you lead (James 3:1, Proverbs 27:23-24).
He cares about how you treat people (Matthew 7:12, Phil 2:3).
He cares about how you grow (1 Timothy 4:8).
He cares about how you spend your weekends (Proverbs 4:23).
He cares about multiplying what you have (Matthew 25:14-30).
He cares about discipleship (Matthew 28:19-20).
He cares about you (Psalm 32:8, 1 Peter 5:6-7).

In marketplace ministry, you have two goals: be successful in business and find opportunities to further your ministry. That's the challenge of marketplace ministry. Your actions in business and ministry must align with the Scriptures and point to your purpose. It means Jesus can join you at church and at work. He can listen in the boardroom, behind closed doors, during negotiations and at lunch. Everywhere you go, He is welcome. It all starts with a firm foundation and actions that connect to purpose.

Your marketplace ministry needs a firm foundation to not only build a legacy but also to maintain a stellar reputation. People need to know you, your business and your ministry. They need to see your heart and the commitment that you bring with every business transaction, every phone call and every sale. When people perceive you correctly, it's a set-up for your marketing, referrals and a successful business and ministry. But it doesn't happen automatically. Being great in your marketplace ministry requires intentionality and principles that govern how you operate.

Here are 8 principles of marketplace ministry to make sure your actions connect to your purpose.

- Have a commitment to excel in business and ministry.
- Create a loving culture in your business and ministry.
- Embrace your freedom to honor God at work.
- Be intentional about developing opportunities for others.
- Have authentic care for business associates and their concerns.
- Encourage spiritual and personal growth for all team members.
- Encourage everyone to make money, be a good steward and use their resources to help others.
- Foster balance and an enjoyment of life and work.

Take a closer look at the above list and add additional statements that apply specifically to your marketplace ministry. Print your list and place it in a prominent place. Read the list often to remind you of your purpose and commitment to honor God, give your best and care for others.

Now that you have some foundational principles in place, let's talk about your personal life. Earlier, you read that Legacy Leaders show biblical character, not only in the workplace but everywhere they go. You might ask, "How can I show biblical character while growing my business to make a profit?" You begin by setting parameters around yourself. Decide now what you will and will not do to make a profit. Yes, you will work hard and efficiently but say, "No," to opportunities that go against the Scriptures. These kinds of situations are tricky. There's nothing wrong with progress and recognition, right? Not so fast. When an opportunity for progress comes, always check for the attachments.

A while back, I signed on with a marketing company for my financial business. The company promised leads and better deals for my clients. They would offer more training, lavish vacations, pay incentives and bonuses. They showed me a path to becoming very wealthy in a much shorter time than I projected. I signed the contract and was all in! A few months later, they made some changes to the contract that only required my initials. The contract signing happened during a hyped-up conference with friends and fun. There was a little voice nudging at me saying, "Rhonda, read the contract updates. Stop and read!" But in all the fun and hype, I ignored the voice and signed. Wow! What a mistake.

The new contract had plenty of bells and whistles. It also had a statement that gave ownership of all new clients to the marketing company. They gave me a few minor gifts but I gave them ownership of my future business! In the financial industry, you have a book of business that is lucrative if you grow it. I have been in the business for over 20 years. A good book of business is a part of my wealth to pass to my children. Instead, the contract gave ownership of the new business to the president of the marketing company. They also wanted me to end my relationships with other companies and only work through them. He was building his own wealth and turning me into what felt like an employee.

Getting out wasn't easy. The fine print also had a non-compete clause, which meant I had to wait two years to re-establish my relationship with the clients I met during my time with that organization. It was a costly mistake that won't happen again.

When I look back, I ask myself, "Why did you sign that contract? Why did you let your guard down so easily?"

The company offered a cocktail of opportunities that I wanted. They even added some language that I value like, purpose and giving back. It sounded good. The people were nice. They made a lot of money and they even talked about God sometimes. They attracted me to an opportunity that I wanted for myself. I let my guard down and didn't count the cost.

Listen. With your marketplace ministry, always count the cost. It doesn't matter who makes the offer. It doesn't matter if they say they love God, too. Even if they say you will make a lot of money and gain notoriety, wait. Read before you sign. You are building a legacy. Always keep the ownership of your business and the rights to what you create. If you sign a contract that gives another person rights, add a clause that gives everything back to you when the collaboration is done. When God blesses your gifts and moves you forward, people want to join the ride.

At this point in your journey, obvious tricks like illegal activity and actions that cause physical harm are usually not tempting. Instead, the enemy will use offers and proposed partnerships that are extremely appealing and seemingly innocent. He will offer something that you want. It will feel right but there will always be a hook in the meat. Something will be off; something will be wrong. When this happens, say "NO" and run! Your desires won't hold out if you stay and gaze. Get out of there!

There is no one who is beyond being intoxicated by the enemy's schemes. Do what Jesus did while being tempted in the wilderness (Matthew 4:1-11). Go to the Word! The enemy is not just after your business or money; he wants your reputation. He wants to end you, your ministry, your family and your legacy.

You will read more about this in Chapter 10: How to Make Your Business Your Ministry – The New Marketplace Ministry.

Understand the importance of reputation and perceptions. How you treat people and the decisions they see you make matters. They will believe what you do much more than what you say. Remember the builder and the splitting foundation? It did not matter what they advertised. The news about the splitting house was the message people received.

Here are seven ways to connect your actions to your purpose and avoid those costly detours:

Avoid nepotism

Yes, hire people you trust but be careful giving favor to family members and overlooking deficiencies and lack of commitment. It will cost you later.

Embrace your community

In marketplace ministry, it is your responsibility to reach beyond your doors and show care to your community. It is not just about profit and how to close the next deal. Your community matters and needs to see that you care.

Be careful how you fire and lay-off people

Try not to fire people without giving them advance notice, severance pay, and help to move forward. Consider how you influence people personally and take an extra step to help them transition and move forward positively. People talk about how you treat them. Send a positive message about your business with the people who leave.

Be honest when you hire people

If the position is uncertain, hire a person from a temporary contract service. If the turnover is high because there's an aspect of the job that's very difficult, tell them the truth and pay them for their trouble. Be Honest About the Challenges of the Position

Demonstrate care for the personal struggles of your employees

Your team needs to know that you care about them beyond their ability to help your business. Some people who work with you are going through difficult situations, yet they still come to work and get the job done. Look for ways to let people know you care about them. Send cards, give gifts, give them unplanned perks (like leaving early) and show up for their special occasions.

Provide equality with pay

This is a major problem, especially for women in the workplace. Don't pay people more because you like them or just because they ask. Develop a salary system based on skills that do not discriminate.

Provide excellent service

This is the way you tell your customer, "You matter." Poor customer service is unacceptable for any business.

Treat everyone with respect

Managers have a higher position in the company but they do not have a higher position with God. Yes, top management makes more money but that does not mean they are better than everyone else. It just means they have a unique skill; their position pays more and has a higher level of responsibility. Value every person, show respect, no matter what position they hold.

In my business, I recall providing financial help to a beautiful lady in her late seventies. She wanted to increase her insurance and change her retirement plans. After a review of everything she had, I saw a big problem in the future with her current plan. I showed her ways to reduce her expenses instead of adding a new plan. I passed on earning the commission to show kindness to a woman who needed help. In marketplace ministry, that's what we do. Our integrity and honesty matter more than money.

The primary goal is to treat people well at every level. Your business is the example of how a company can be successful without compromising biblical values. Everyone on your staff should grow, learn and get better. The day your business stops growing is the day your business starts dying.

Now that you see a big picture of how you treat people in a marketplace ministry, it's time to create a foundation for your ministry.

Statement of Faith

The Statement of Faith helps you maintain consistency in your decision-making and goal-setting. A Statement of Faith is not only helpful for people who work with you, it also helps lay a foundation to keep your organization on track.

The statement doesn't have to list everything you believe but it should state the foundational truths that govern your marketplace ministry. These are your spiritual commitments that are non-negotiable. They are truths that will never change. The reason this is so important is that as circumstances change, your Statement of Faith will be your guide to help you easily say, "No," to some opportunities while you embrace other opportunities. As you set goals, the Statement of Faith serves as a reminder of your foundational faith commitments.

Start by reading the doctrinal statement of your church and other ministries that you appreciate. Now, think about what matters most to you and the non-negotiable biblical truths that you must include. Our Statement of Faith is short but it includes our foundational, biblical absolutes and reminds us of our commitment to care for others and honor God in all that we do. All our business and workplace activities agree with these standards.

Your Statement does not have to be long, just accurate and well crafted. Be sure to include information that is relevant for your business and your commitment to serve others. When you are done, place your Statement of Faith in a prominent place and review it at selected times.

Here is the Statement of Faith from Ministry in Business:

Statement of Faith

On each of these beliefs, we will not bend.

1. We believe that God created the heavens, the earth and all living things, including human beings. Science, the valid study of God's handiwork, ultimately points to God.
2. We believe there is only one God, revealed as Father, Son and Holy Spirit (Deuteronomy 6:4, 2 Corinthians 13:14, John 1:1).
3. We believe that our Lord Jesus Christ was begotten, not created, truly God and truly Man. He was born of the Virgin Mary, lived a sinless life, died a vicarious and atoning death for the sins of the world, resurrected bodily for our justification and now reigns in glory until all things are put under His feet (1 Timothy 3:16).
4. We believe that man was made in the image of God and is the crown of creation. By reason of the fall, we became spiritually depraved and alienated from our creator (Psalm 8, Ephesians 2:8-9).
5. We believe that justification happens by grace through faith in Jesus Christ's sacrifice on Calvary (Romans 3:21 – 24). This opportunity is available for everyone for as long as they have breath.

6. We believe the Holy Spirit dwells in all believers, conforming them to the image of Jesus Christ (1 Corinthians 12:13, Romans 8:16-17). The Holy Spirit is active within the Body of Christ until the coming of the Lord. We believe the development of all spiritual gifts should be encouraged preparing you to serve fellow Christ-followers and to go out and do the ministry for which you were called (Acts 8:14-17, Acts 19:1-2, 1 Corinthians 12:4-7)

7. We believe in the absolute inspiration of the Holy Scriptures, given by the Holy Spirit, without error. Furthermore, we believe that no individual or organization has the authority to establish doctrine contrary to the Scriptures, which were subsequently accepted as canon by the early Christian Church (2 Timothy 3:16). The Holy Bible is God's Word, written by men who were inspired by the Holy Spirit.

8. We believe in the literal second coming of our Lord, the literal rule of Christ upon the earth and the ultimate victory of the eternal Kingdom of God (Acts 1:9-11), Daniel 12:2, Revelation 22:1-7).

Reflections for My Wild Friends

God does not deal in single generations. He is a legacy God who connects bloodlines from generation to generation. What you do affects your children and grandchildren. If you clear a path to success, your children get to walk on it with more ease than you experienced. If you leave a path of despair and brokenness, they must do the work of clearing the debris to start with a fresh legacy. The wonder of God's work shines when generation upon generation walks with God, optimizing purpose and multiplying the legacy.

It is beautiful to see God's hand on a sold-out believer who is anchored in Him setting the stage for generations to come. Pray for

God to anchor you and commit to the lifetime journey of pursuing Him. Let God amaze you!

Five

ACTIVATE - Connect Your Purpose to Your Ministry

"In marketplace ministry, everything matters - the surrounding people, your words and the actions you take."

In my early Christian journey, I attended a small church start-up in Houston, Texas. With about 60 members, we met in a school on Sundays and in homes during the week. Some of the best relationships I have ever experienced happened during my time at Friendship Community Bible Church. We didn't just go to church together; we hung out together, went on vacations, shared holidays and spent many weekends playing spades and Phase 10.

One Sunday, we arrived for church service and the door was bolted. The person who opens the building was not there. The building was dark and cold. We stood outside, puzzled but thinking the person who normally unlocked the door had an emergency and couldn't make it. When we finally reached the school administrator, he said, "Didn't you get the message? You can't meet here anymore."

"No, we didn't get the message. So, you can't allow us to meet but you forgot to tell us?" Standing in front of the school in shock, about thirty of us gathered for prayer. By then, it was 12:00 pm and church normally started at 11:00 am. As time passed, it slowly sank in our mind that church would not happen. We stood in dismay in the school parking lot uncertain about the future of our church. The relationships were rich and the commitments were firm but our small church didn't have the money to secure a new place to meet.

Monday, Tuesday, then Wednesday came and we still didn't have a place to meet. Finally, Thursday the word was out, we signed a lease on a new place to meet! Some of our members came together with a deposit from their personal bank accounts, securing our new space by Friday.

The decorators in our church brought beautiful décor from their homes. Members who were business owners donated supplies, a sound system and everything we needed for the children's ministry, choir and the pulpit area. When it looked like there was no hope, God orchestrated a powerful comeback. Our small congregation refused to sit back and witness the end of their local church. They aligned themselves with a common goal and pooled their resources. With unity and alignment, by Sunday, the church doors opened again. What a privilege to worship God who provided a bigger and better space. Friendship Community Bible Church is still thriving over 35 years later. What looked like the end turned into a new beginning. It wasn't just the alignment with each other but also God's perfect timing to activate the ministry at a new level.

In the Bible, Joseph (Genesis 37, 39–50) operated with excellence in an environment that did not agree with his faith. He is the great example of a marketplace minister who unapologetically worshiped the one true God. He used his spiritual gifts in a pagan environment and God favored and protected him, his family and his people. When you are called to marketplace ministry, God creates a pathway for your ministry to flourish, no matter where you operate.

Through Joseph's life, the Bible teaches two overarching lessons that show how a marketplace minister should function.

1. A marketplace minister uses spiritual gifts in the workplace.
2. A marketplace minister also optimizes natural talent in the workplace. This includes natural talents that people use in everyday life, like playing music, singing, communicating, art, managing numbers and athletic ability.

Finishing what God is calling you to accomplish requires your gifts and talents to be used fully. Your faith enhances what you do when your goal is to honor God. Let people see you excel and lead the way in business. Make yourself so valuable in your position that people listen because they respect your business ability.

Genesis 41:14 begins the story of Joseph and his dream about a famine coming to Egypt. The Pharaoh charged Joseph with developing a plan to make sure Egypt survived the famine. Joseph exceeded the Pharaoh's request and saved his own people. Through Joseph's leadership, they didn't just survive the famine but they thrived during the famine. Joseph used strategic business principles that brought profit and favor to Egypt. He also respected the person in authority, even though he did not serve the one true God. Joseph did what was right because that was his job. He made himself so valuable that the Pharaoh promoted him to the highest position next to himself.

Before you set up your marketplace ministry, read about the life of Joseph and look for ways to align your life and decisions with this great man of faith.

"Whatever you do, do your work heartily, as for the Lord rather than for men." (Colossians 3:23)

In Chapter 4, your goal was to write your Statement of Faith. The next step is to consider how you will activate your spiritual gifts and talents in your business and ministry. Let's reflect on a few questions to make sure your ministry and business are properly aligned.

Will you have a for-profit business that integrates ministry into the daily business?

For example:

- Insurance agencies, realtors, tax and financial professionals
- Restaurants, food trucks and other eating establishments
- Stores, sales reps or retail business owners
- Service establishments, hairstylists, car care and other repair services
- Part-time workers (ride share, food delivery, etc)
- Writer, artist, speaker
- Jewelry, and multi-level marketing sales

Will you work as an employee in an office or from home?

- Accountants
- Customer service representatives
- City workers

- Lawyers and doctors
- Managers, general office work

Will you work primarily in a ministry?

- Pastor, Bible study teacher, counselor
- Church worker
- Missionary

Follow the next three steps to determine the direction for your alignment.

#1 Clearly define your business and your ministry in a simple statement. For example:

I am an educator with a gift of teaching, discipleship and evangelism. I use my gifts in my business and ministry by providing smart insurance and retirement solutions for seniors, families and professionals. I also teach Bible study, speak and develop written and digital content.

#2 Get the licenses, training and certifications needed for your marketplace ministry.

Your marketplace ministry can begin by simply praying for people or working in an area that requires training, licenses and certifications. If it takes time to get the qualifications you need, find a place to start while you work on what you need.

#3 Define what ministry you will offer. Look for opportunities to connect with people who will benefit from what you are offering.

Marketplace ministry is all about influencing people. To be effective, think about how and where you will connect with the right people.

Will you get to know people during lunch?

Will you show kindness while you are doing your job?

Will you meet people through an organization or club?

There are many ways to make connections. Spend some time in prayer and ask God to guide you to the right people and help you make good connections. He loves when you are ready to make Him known.

#4 Choose the best business structure.

Since a marketplace ministry is a business, you must select a business structure for tax purposes. Begin with deciding if you will be for profit or a non-profit 501 (c)(3). This is one of the most important financial decisions you will make for your marketplace ministry. The costs associated with benefits, salaries and programs are a challenge. Let's face it, money is a big deal. It's at the center of operations for business and ministry. That's why the 501 (c)(3) tax status is the popular way to organize a ministry because of the tax deduction. Ministries look to donors to provide for ministry operations, salaries and missions. Donors enjoy the tax deduction for their donations. The IRS code gives you tax advantages for operating a non-profit organization with the 501(c)(3) status but it also has limitations. For some ministries, it's the only structure that makes sense but for others, there is a better option.

I favor a for-profit status whenever possible because the non-profit status limits some functions, including how you dissolve the organization. That means you build it for the community and when you retire, you can't transfer the organization and its holdings to your children as part of your estate. Instead, it goes to another non-profit organization that represents the community. The 501(c)(3) status also has limitations on activities such as earning income, political involvement, selling goods and transferring assets. It continues to face political challenges that will probably lead to drastic changes in the future.

Wild friends, if you will step out of the box and run your ministry differently, you can make the money you need and support your ministry. A for-profit organization enjoys more freedom but also pays taxes on earnings. It's worth it when you are free to earn as much money as your ability allows. By removing the limitations, you can earn your income *and* fulfill your ministry purpose at the same time.

Think about it. A for-profit marketplace ministry allows you to be an example for people to see by your actions, not just your words. People need to see your financial strength and biblical lifestyle on stage, in media, education, finance and any business you choose. Enjoy a comfortable lifestyle. Be active and visible in your community. Allow your business to create a hedge to help you thrive in your ministry through inflation, challenges and unexpected events like Covid-19. A for-profit marketplace ministry gives you the opportunity to make enough money to support yourself, your ministry and any additional organizations that you want to support. Yes, you will pay taxes but the freedom you get in return is worth it.

Benefits of a "For-Profit" Marketplace Ministry

- You will be above reproach when asked about your spending. You can respond with something like, "I don't take an income from the giving, my income comes from my earnings."

- Your taxable income gives you the freedom to transfer wealth and assets to your children.
- A for-profit status allows you to bless your ministry and other people in any way you chose.
- A for-profit status allows you to use all your abilities, in and out of ministry, to support your ministry and your family.
- Successful for-profit organizations gain respect in the business world, adding a new level to your ministry opportunities, relationships and influence.
- People don't decide how much money you make through their giving. You decide how much you make through your work and diligence.
- The business world offers unlimited income.
- When you hire people for your marketplace ministry, you provide greater earning opportunities for others.
- You show a biblical lifestyle in the marketplace as you interact through your business.
- As a successful business, you can give more than most people.
- You will enjoy a personal lifestyle without as many questions about personal assets and spending.
- Other ministries that can't adapt to this format need your contributions.
- You will pay your staff well and offer better benefits.
- You will be a better ministry example and influence your community.
- You won't have the rules and regulations that limit your freedoms.

In a for-profit ministry, you are a smart person with business and money-making skills, yet you submit to God for guidance. Your career approach considers people over profits. Although you have the skills to maneuver the corporate world, you still care wholeheartedly about God's agenda. You are bold enough to go hard to make money and go hard after God's plan for your life and your money. You are free to enjoy life and money, yet your greatest joy is not money and prestige but giving and influencing people for Jesus Christ.

Benefits of the Non-Profit Status

Of course, there are benefits to having a 501(c)(3) and reasons that you should consider. It makes sense for churches because of the large population of givers and other benefits and responsibilities. They need it for missions and organizations called to impoverished areas with limited resources and opportunities. Some large donors only give if you have the 501(c)(3) status.

Other Tax Benefits

Weigh this decision carefully. There is not a cookie-cutter design that's right for everyone. Some organizations choose a dual set-up with two separate organizations. The non-profit organization serves missions and other needs, such as disadvantaged populations, scholarships and programs. The for-profit organization creates business opportunities and higher income earning potential. Donors appreciate knowing their giving goes to people in need and programs instead of mostly salaries and buildings. The ministry leader can also flourish by the increased income opportunity that a business provides. Marketplace ministry extends your reach with limitless possibilities.

Whatever you choose, it's good to talk to an attorney to help decide what's best for you and your organization. Don't stop short by just watching what other people are doing. Do your research, then chose what's best for you and the work that God is calling you to finish. Remember, in marketplace ministry, you don't have to choose ministry or business; you can have both.

Only certain people are wild enough to establish a business as a financial source for ministry. It's not for everyone. But if you know God created you with a wild desire to be different, look closer at your options and turn your passion into money and ministry. Through your business, seek creative ways to support the ministry and earn a good living for yourself. Let me clarify. It is right to pay people who serve in ministry. There are several examples in the Bible that direct us to give to those who serve in ministry (1 Timothy 5:18, Luke 10:7). This book focuses on those who serve in business and are also called by God.

You may ask, "Can a business be a ministry?" The answer is, "Absolutely!" Just because you make money doesn't mean you have to abandon purpose and genuinely caring for people. Ministries function as businesses in many ways. A ministry keeps up with the administration of the organization and people get paid, just like a business. Ministries also show accountability for money handling and the hiring and firing of people. While the goals and visions of ministry and business are different, some day-to-day activities are very similar.

Wild friends let's get a broader perspective. Money gives you options and increased ability to influence (when you are a good steward), right? So, yes! Make money but be generous with your money. Throw away the idea that your giving goal stops at 10%; biblically that is the minimum. Plan to make enough money to give more out of your other 90%. It already belongs to God. Instead, give freely from your own increase. Let your marketplace ministry shine in your community and beyond, then watch what investing in God's kingdom yields.

Activating Your Ministry and Business

A business makes a profit for the sake of profit, growth, power and position. It has an agenda that is usually in line with the owner, board, stockholders and executives. A ministry cares about growth as well but has a deeper purpose and seeks to honor God first. The ministry can have executives but to stay true to the purpose and call of the organization, everyone who is a part of the ministry should agree with the biblical standards of the ministry. To say it better, a marketplace ministry takes the aspects of a business and governs everything by biblical principles and God's agenda.

Making your business your ministry happens, not only because of your product but because of You. In a marketplace ministry, you run a honest business but also show your commitment to care about people and draw them into a personal faith journey. A ministry cares for and supports people as a priority, even when business challenges arise. Your foundational ministry commitments do not change because of a need to increase revenue. Yes, you need money to keep the doors open but you have more to consider before you decide how to respond. Your decisions are not just about money. You also must think about the commitments in your Statement of Faith, your purpose for the ministry and other goals. Instead of following normal business tactics, use your creativity, gifts, talents and prayer to find solutions that keep your ministry and business aligned with God's plan and your purpose.

As stated earlier, I have a ministry called Ministry In Business (MIB). I also own a business. My goal is to empty myself of every gift God has given me. All the activities can make money and they all have a ministry function. At start-up, my business paid for the supplies and administrative costs of my ministry, including my website, designers and digital services. While I am free to offer products at a cost, my ministry will not go away if people don't buy a product. There is no financial stress in my ministry. We don't need to find donors because the business provides for the ministry. It is the financial safety net for my personal finances and the ministry. While some ministries will always need donors, look for opportunities to create a hedge for your personal finances. It makes it much easier when change occurs.

My marketplace ministry friends, it is always ministry *and* business. We bring sincerity and honesty to every meeting and we are diligent with our work and business goals. We are builders who believe most of our business ventures have a money-making component *and* a ministry goal. As the business grows, so does the ministry. Your setup may be different but whatever you decide, don't compromise on what matters – finishing what God calls you to accomplish. I am glad you are not sitting on the sidelines watching other people in ministry and business. I am so glad you are in the game!

"But you are a chosen race, a royal priesthood, a holy nation, a people for God's own possession, so that you may proclaim the excellencies of Him who has called you out of darkness into His marvelous light." (1 Peter 2:9)

Reflections for my Wild Friends

A ministry does not have to be a non-profit but if it works for you, the advantages are many. It all depends on your goals and how you operate. The big picture goal is to use, build and multiply every gift and talent that God gives you. (Read Matthew 25:14-30.)

Out of ten non-profit organizations I've been close to, only three were in good shape financially. Those three organizations have unlimited financial resources because of their connections to givers in the business community. Of course, that's not normal. Many non-profit organizations and churches struggle financially and consider fundraising as the major challenge of the organization. For them, and many others, the only way to survive is through donor giving. That means if, through legislation, the requirements to keep the non-profit status change, the ministry would be in trouble or at least have some major decisions to make.

If you can avoid it, I believe it's better to find another way to fund your personal income. However, if you choose to go the non-profit route, there are a few points to consider.

- Spend plenty of time praying and reflecting on the purpose of your ministry to stay within your planned parameters.
- Refer to your Statement of Faith regularly and don't compromise.
- Create and implement a funding plan that defines how to attract donors.
- Don't wait until you have your non-profit to serve. Start now so you can learn valuable lessons that you will need later.

Please don't allow these steps to overwhelm you. If you have a heart to serve and you're ready, go for it and take your steps one day at a time. The main point is that you don't have to live beneath your capabilities just because you work for a ministry. You can do both. Use your ministry gifts and your talents in the business world. Make them both advance God's plan for your life. Remember, you can ask for contributions, even without the 501(c)(3). The benefit of the 501(c)(3) is the tax deduction. A tax deduction is a bonus given by the government, not a requirement for a sincere gift from the heart.

Six

Advance - Connect Your Ministry to Your Business

"It's better to stay in the battle, even when it's tough, than not to fight at all. Fight until you win."

Everyone gets a certain number of heartbeats at birth. Those heartbeats have a start date and an end date. The real action happens in the middle. I like to call the space in middle the great equalizer. It does not matter how much money you have or who you know. The great equalizer is the truth that everyone has a date with destiny where you give an account for how you lived. It happens after you experience your last heartbeat (Romans 14:12). With that sobering truth in mind, every minute of your life matters. You don't have time to waste on meaningless activities that drain your energy and waste your valuable time. Life is too important to give away your heartbeats to activities that lead you away from your goals and add nothing to your life. Everyone should find something that adds purpose and meaning to your life.

The good news is that if you are reading this book, you still have time to make your heartbeats matter. Your marketplace ministry needs you, not later but now. As a follower of Christ, you have a biblical mandate to be an example for the world to see. That does not mean that you force-feed people the gospel. It means that people around you don't have to look very far to see a biblical lifestyle. They can simply observe you and see a picture of how God wants them to live. Activating your marketplace ministry is that easy. Just let people see you! Let your life be your testimony. Take the next steps, give yourself time to grow, seize your opportunity and activate!

The next step to activate your marketplace ministry depends on where you are now. If you already have a business or career but want to make it your ministry, then you have some specific steps to take. Remember, a marketplace ministry is not just a ministry. It's not just a business either. It's both. That means you must figure out how to make money and how to honor God with the money you have. A business that is also a marketplace ministry is required to operate like a regular business while honoring God in the daily commitments and activities. You advertise, offer a product, sell, take care of customers and pay taxes. You also pray, treat people the way God wants you to and live in a way that honors God.

Accomplishments at this level are not random. Instead, they are driven by deep inner commitments and beliefs. There is a reason marketplace ministry is interesting to you. To build and multiply, your reason "why" must withstand opinions, attacks and everything that tries to stop you. Your reason makes you different, a little wild and open to seeing things God's way. Establishing the why for your marketplace ministry will keep you going when you don't see the rewards, when you are tired and when attacks come against you.

This inner drive won't let you go; I tried it. If you stop, it will keep pulling you back. It's better to stay in the fight and keep trying than not to fight at all. Lots of people start but only the wild friends finish. You finish because you learn to honor God over people. You finish because you know why you do what you do. Your why gives you a purpose that's more than just making money. It makes every day, every battle, worth it.

Knowing the reason why drives you forward. You keep going because you know life is short and you want every day to matter. You are aware of your heartbeats and the limited time you have to complete your God-given purpose on earth. This awareness sets you up for marketplace ministry. As you design and activate your business, every action points back to your why. Whatever you do every day, find a reason why you do it.

Writing and Activating Your Marketplace Ministry Business Plan

Now that you understand your why, let's talk about what you want. The best way to organize any business is with a business plan. A marketplace ministry business plan is like a general business plan. I suggest you visit the United States Small Business Administration website, where you will find valuable information to help you write a business plan (sba.gov).

On this site, you will find information to help you select the legal structure for your business (sole proprietorship, partnership, LLC or corporation) and the vital parts of a business plan. Write details about your commitment to marketplace ministry and how that will happen in the Executive Summary and Organizational and Management section of the business plan.

To incorporate your ministry into your business plan, go back to your why. For example, if you feel a desire to help people, how will you help people in your business? Will you offer a service, prayer, kind words or meet a need? Include every detail in the management section of your business plan. Revisit your statement several times and be sure that every goal aligns with your ministry Statement of Faith and your why statement.

Here are a few examples of how other business owners created a marketplace ministry statement in their business plan.

- A photographer writes, "I help people tell their story by capturing splendid memories."
- An educator writes, "I shape futures and open minds to new possibilities."
- An entertainer writes, "I help people smile, even when they don't feel like it."
- A businessperson writes, "I provide jobs for families to live better."
- An evangelist writes, "I help people find rest for their soul today and assurance for their soul's future."
- A therapist writes, "I help people live better."
- A restaurant owner writes, "I create amazing meals that warm the heart and nourish the body."
- A realtor writes, "I help people get closer to financial wellness by owning a home."
- A driver writes, "I give people meaningful, encouraging conversations when they ride with me."
- A speaker writes, "I deliver inspiring messages that draw people into a closer relationship with Jesus Christ."

There is harmony between business and ministry when you operate without compromising your spiritual commitments. To make sure you stay on the right track, also create a solid Mission Statement and Vision Statement for your marketplace ministry.

The Mission Statement tells what your marketplace ministry does and defines how you will reach your objectives. It states the action that will happen because of your ministry's purpose.

The Vision Statement acts as an inspiring guiding statement that summarizes what the organization hopes to achieve in the future.

Sample Mission Statement

To provide our clients with innovative financial solutions tailored to their needs and goals through expert guidance, enduring relationships, exceptional service and world class investment and money management strategies.

Sample Vision Statement

Our business demonstrates a God-given gift of encouragement used to help people achieve their goals. The foundational platform of our organization is rooted in education, relationships, integrity and purpose. Our atmosphere is professional, with high energy and exceptional optimism. We are leaders in our business and our community. We are "out-of-the-box" thinkers who put the needs of others ahead of our own when it promotes God's agenda. Together, we celebrate victories and join hands through challenges. We are purposeful, bold and courageous.

More to Consider for Your Business

Learn about business legal requirements for your state, county and city. Learn about handling taxes and record-keeping. Become familiar with the U.S. Small Business Administration website at SBA.gov.

Think about funding. Where will you get the money to start your business?

Where will you operate your business, at home, storefront or will you need office space?

How will the business make money?

What expenses will you incur?

How will you find customers?

Who will manage your website, social media and marketing?

How will you personalize your business to make it different from your competitors?

Another source to help answer these questions and launch the business part of your ministry is Score.org. They offer workshops, mentors and other tools to help business owners.

Every business has meaningful opportunities if people are around. You can make someone's day better with encouragement, prayer or sometimes just being good company. Take a step back and think about the opportunities that allow your business to influence people. What can you do with the opportunities that you have? Find your marketplace ministry statement by answering your own questions and discovering how you help others find solutions for their problems. The best source to discover what works best is knowing your spiritual gifts and how to use them.

Your Spiritual Gifts

Your spiritual gifts are a golden ticket for operating your marketplace ministry. When your gifts are active, people need you around because they benefit from your gifts. You also find more comfort in your day-to-day responsibilities. It's like being at home, even if you are working hard and life is not perfect. Being connected and using your gifts gives you a peace that you don't find in other places. Operating in your gifts also gives you more energy and patience.

They don't wear you out like other activities, even when you are tired. No matter what you do, your gifts will always look for an opportunity to be used. You know when it happens because it feels like home.

A few years ago, I worked a contract as a human resources manager. I oversaw a major lay-off and closing of a data center. The home office hired me to manage the process smoothly and with no drama. They gave me specific instructions not to discuss the details of the lay-off with anyone. Even the branch manager was unaware of the details of my six-month assignment.

In the beginning, there was nothing said or asked about my position or why they hired me. After a few weeks, I made new friends. The branch manager was a very likable man and cared about his job and employees. I met people in the data center and listened as they discussed their plans and goals. They learned about my faith and started asking questions about the Bible. My relationships became authentic, even to the point of sharing my faith and offering guidance to some workers. However, as time passed, they started asking questions. They wanted to know, "Why are you here?"

The branch manager started hearing rumors and finally asked me, "What do you know?" This is where two opposing forces met: my commitment to God and my commitment to my employer. They both deserved the best from me. However, only one force is King. A commitment to God always takes precedence over other areas, even when they are good.

I have spiritual gifts, which include exhortation and evangelism. While I was moving around the center, meeting people and building relationships, I wasn't just the new HR manager. I was a lady with a gift of evangelism and exhortation quietly operating in a management role. At the core, the activation of the gifts is a driving force that is hard to hide. Your gifts show up somewhere in your life, even if you do not use them for the right reasons.

After a few weeks, I did what I believed was right. First, I confided in the branch manager so he could make personal plans. Then, I gave the workers enough information for them the start making plans. I recall one young lady sharing the good news that she was going to buy her first car in a few days and was nervous about the financial commitment. She was so excited about her big step, and I didn't want to burst her bubble but I asked her to wait a week before making the purchase. I knew she would not have a job the following week.

The layoff happened. I closed a building that had 300 employees, turned off the lights and left. The leader in me sincerely desired to complete the contract as instructed. But when my spiritual identity kicked in and activated my spiritual gifts, I decided to handle the situation differently. Yes, I executed the layoff but I did not keep the secret. Instead, I created a better experience for the people who were being laid off. I always wondered if the company knew I didn't keep their secret. However, it really doesn't matter, it was a risk that the marketplace minister in me had to take.

After that experience, I reflected on what happened. Ideally, it was my responsibility to follow the contract as instructed but I just couldn't do it. That experience taught me to never take a job or contract that violates my core beliefs. I can't keep a secret that hurts people, not when I can do something about it. In marketplace ministry, sometimes you must make tough decisions. The best way to avoid the conflict is to be careful what you agree to. Sometimes, you just have to say, "no," even if the money is good. Sometimes, it's not worth the compromise.

Spiritual Gifts at Work

It's important to know your spiritual gifts before you start your marketplace ministry. Then you can align your ministry gifts with your business. The right business creates opportunities for your ministry and your ministry creates opportunities for your gifts. For example, my primary gifts are exhortation, teaching and discipleship. My business encounters open doors for all three gifts to be used. As I stated earlier, we spend most of our time during the week working. The significant benefit of marketplace ministry is that you are free to earn the money that you need while doing the ministry that you love. Going to work? Take your ministry with you and add value to your work every day. Don't wait for an event or for someone to acknowledge you before using your spiritual gifts. The wait is over. The time is now!

Using your gifts in your business doesn't happen because you make an announcement or hang a sign on your wall. It also doesn't happen because you speak some cliche church words on unsuspecting people. Your gifts activate through actions that are guided by God. Spiritual gifts, when used correctly, are priceless to the person who benefits. Your gifts bring unity, equip the church and serve people for the better good.

If you have a gift of helps, people call you very thoughtful and always willing the assist.

If you have a gift of teaching, they see you as the person who explains new procedures clearly.

The gift of exhortation will manifest as an encourager or cheerleader who helps people advance.

The gift of discipleship shows up in people who are great mentors and people who interns hope to work with.

A gift of pastor will show up in excellent executive leaders. They may not hold the office of pastor but a good leader finds ways to lead and use the gift in the work environment.

"Whoever speaks, is to do so as one who is speaking the utterances of God; whoever serves is to do so as one who is serving by the strength which God supplies; so that in all things God may be glorified through Jesus Christ, to whom belongs the glory and dominion forever and ever." (1 Peter 4:11)

Every gift has a place to function and there are no limitations on where your gift can shine. That's why you can't wait to find a place in your local church to use your gift. Yes, it's important to serve in the local church but it's not the only place where followers of Christ are called to serve. Instead of just serving inside of the building, many of us are called to serve outside of the building or both. Marketplace ministry extends the church outside of the walls. You don't have to wait to go to church to use your gifts. Find a good Bible teaching church to attend where relationships are rich and the leaders are authentic; but also look for opportunities that God is providing, right where you are.

Bringing it All Together

When you know why marketplace ministry is important, you bring it all together by writing a plan and using your spiritual gifts. You must bring your "A" game like a true wild friend. Start with a bold stance that is willing to do what others won't. Make a commitment to adjust when needed without deviating from the course. Your "A" game also means managing the ups and down of your business and ministry without compromising your non-negotiables.

Stick with your original commitment

When you incorporate marketplace ministry into your business, you make a commitment to create ways to honor God in your business. Honoring God means caring about people. So, when you can make more money but it requires you to deviate slightly from putting God first you say, "No." Stick with the original plan and put God first, even if it costs you.

And let us not grow weary of doing good, for in due season we will reap, if we do not give up (Galatians 6:9).

Be courageous

Once you are successful in your business and ministry, it's likely that you will encounter someone who wants to discredit you. A strategy of the enemy, when he can't stop you, is to try to stop people from believing in you and eventually make you stop yourself. No matter what other people say or do, stick with the plan and take your battles to God. If He led you to start a marketplace ministry, trust Him to protect it and help you keep it.

Authentically care for others

It's easy to focus so intently on growth that you forget about the importance of how you treat people. When you mistreat people, your business may be successful but you pay a price in lost relationships and poor reputation. *A mark of marketplace ministry is caring for people.* Take the time needed to listen and let your customers and your team know they matter. Authentic relationships are the cornerstones that open the door to show God's love.

This is my commandment, that you love one another,
as I have loved you." (John15:12)

Embrace a lifestyle of prayer

When you operate a ministry and a business, you are going against the normal business culture and it will require a lifestyle of prayer to press forward. In marketplace ministry, you make decisions based on the Bible instead of profits. You move in directions based on God's guidance instead of trends. Every decision you make requires prayer.

Plan to be the best

A marketplace ministry sets the example of excellence in business. If there are sales quotas, break a records! If you have business goals, exceed the expectation. Be clean in your management and wise in your growth strategies. Be so authentic in business that people want to know more about you and your faith.

An effective marketplace ministry is an influential organization. To influence people requires that you are more than just talk. People need to see that what you say works in your life. Your marketplace ministry is a business designed to house a ministry opportunity. Use your passion in your business and let your business support your passion. Align your business and ministry with complementary goals and connect with people who have similar commitments. When you are this perfectly aligned with your "A" game, God can do amazing work through you.

Your job is much more important than just the obvious reason that people pay you. Anyone can sell a house or style your hair. However, it takes a special person to engage in a meaningful conversation that helps shape your life. In every career, every job, every profession, there are needs beyond profits and products. It could involve a relationship, money, health, stress, loneliness, disappointment and hurt over a loss. You can find a solution that goes beyond what people buy. Find out what keeps a person up at night and how your why meets their needs. Then, make the move that catapults your marketplace ministry forward.

Still not sure how to advance? For some people, it's easy. You know what you want and you know why you want it. For others, you know you want to do something but the details are foggy. You can't decide on *how* to activate your marketplace ministry. Answer this question to help you find the answer that activates your marketplace ministry and helps you connect to the right people.

"What business opportunity puts me in a position to use my spiritual gifts and talents?"

One of the benefits of having a marketplace ministry is having a platform for your spiritual gifts to go forth. It's your innate gifts from God that make you desire to do something special, beyond just making money. It is the reason you can make millions of dollars and not find peace. Those gifts in you yearn to be used and satisfied. You were born with a purpose that needs to be fulfilled.

In business, measures of success are business profits, new clients and people reached. When you connect your marketplace ministry, your measure of success expands to include people that you influence or help. Making money is great but if you do not cultivate meaningful relationships and life purpose, the money will not be enough. Do the work required and ask God to help you attract people to your business and ministry. He's the one who opens ears to hear truth and to understand the scriptures. Get started but give yourself time to learn as you advance.

Strategies for Advancing

During my early days as a Christ follower, I expected way too much from people. I didn't understand how to handle the spiritual warfare that confronted me. I remember my friend telling me, "Look at the writing on the wall." I refused to believe what I did not want to happen. But I learned that refusing to believe did not make it untrue.

In life, we experience good, bad, hurt, joy, pain and comfort. It is all a part of living on earth and sharing life with other people.

"But I say to you, love your enemies and pray for those who persecute you, so that you may prove yourselves to be sons of your Father who is in heaven; for He causes His sun to rise on the evil and the good, and sends rain on the righteous and the unrighteous." (Matthew 5:44-45)

Obstacles happen in your personal life and they happen in marketplace ministry just like any other organization. Be certain of your direction and turn away from everything else. We should align opportunities with our belief in God and His guidance. If you believe God is leading you, draw closer. If He is not, stay away. Everything that leads you somewhere other than where God is leading you is not good for you. To overcome these hinderances, get used to saying "No" and practicing ways to avoid these hindering obstacles.

There are two options that will arise as you advance and face challenges. Both will require prayer and careful consideration. First, sometimes the solution to your problem is to press harder no matter how challenging your situation becomes. Second, sometimes a challenge legitimately leads you in a new direction and a new way to advance.

How do you know the difference?

The best way to govern change is by following a clear roadmap allowing the scriptures to guide you. That is where you get clear guidance about biblical principles to help you make business, ministry and personal decisions. It's like your personal treasure map. You have a starting point, which is where you are now and you have an end goal, which is what God wants you to be. Please notice that the goal is where God wants you to be, not where you decide you want to be. The best plans happen when you want what God wants. As you advance, God will reveal more of His plan. Some experiences will differ from what you expected. You will have options that you didn't expect and you will have important decisions to make.

For example, what should you do when you feel certain that you are on the right path but it is more difficult that you imagined? You want to seize your opportunity but the opportunity seems to slip away. This is not an indicator that it is time to change. Pressure is a part of the process. Notice I did not say stress; pressure happens. It squeezes you to an uncomfortable place, then it forces more ability out of you and expands your capacity. Then after a while, it does not feel like pressure; it feels like life. On the other side, some obstacles are not just pressure, they are doorways. They force you out of old comfortable places and catapult you forward to alternative places that you can't see from the old angle. The key is knowing the difference between a catapult opportunity and a capacity building opportunity. It is importable to learn to navigate both situations as you advance in your marketplace ministry.

- Take a strong stand against destructive words that do not support your goals.
- Pray for God to reveal any deceit.
- Pray before you hire or partner with anyone.

- Pray, fast and meditate about your direction. Stay aligned with the scriptures.
- Do not talk too much. Do not give people ammunition to use against you.
- Pay attention to those "little feelings" you get about people. Take some time to see if the Holy Spirit is giving you a warning to be careful or stay away all together.
- Stay in alignment with God's Word and the direction that He gives you.

Matthew 7:6 says, "Do not give what is holy to dogs, and do not throw your pearls before swine, or they will trample them under their feet, and turn and tear you to pieces."

Good advice from the right person is priceless and hard to find. Poor advice from the wrong person is cheap and easy to find. When you see an obstacle, move away quickly. If you think you do not have any obstacles, look again. They are great at staying hidden until the damage is done. The sooner you recognize and deal with a problem, the sooner you get on with reaching your goal.

The reason it is so important to recognize the trap of hidden obstacles is because making your ministry your business always requires more than you think. That's because advancing a market-place ministry will stretch you. You will take positions on topics that people will not understand. For example, on my website, when you read my posts, it is easy to see that I favor a ministry tax set-up that is for profit. People occasionally email me to challenge the idea of a for-profit ministry. After all, God doesn't care about money, right? My position is, "Wrong!" There are too many Bible verses that mention money handling to say that God doesn't care about it. My position is that the tax status doesn't have to dictate the activity, at least not all of it. That's a stand that I lean into, even though it's difficult for some people to understand.

The greatest success stories do not happen by accident. They happen to people who dare to be different and continue to advance every detail required to reach their goal. These wild friends are so focused that they create their own momentum and withstand the pressure of the opposition. Instead of making excuses, decide that nothing will stop you. At the core of advancing into the details of your goals, develop an unrelenting commitment to press forward, not letting anything stop you. You win, not because you start off being the best but because you refuse to give up in the middle. You advance until you finish. Yes, you may be a little wild but it's okay. Your wild energy is just what God wants to get the job done.

Advancing requires you to make some smart strategic decisions. Be teachable and open to getting help from available and reliable sources. Search the internet and find people sharing about their experience in your area. Listen to podcasts. Attend webinars. Look for a community of people who are successful in your area of interest. Find helpful YouTube channels. Follow a Facebook group and read books that relate to your subject.

When I started writing this book, I wanted to know what mistakes other authors made. I started researching authors and reading their stories. Learning from the mistakes of other people helped me avoid many mistakes. I started with 500 internet subscribers from grassroots writing and speaking. All I knew was that I had a message that needed to be told. Although I had a lot to learn and made some costly mistakes; I kept writing, talking and growing. Looking back, I should have listened to the right people more and the wrong people less. The good news is it's not too late. We should never stop learning.

What happened because of procrastination, poor decisions and not whole-heartedly advancing? There were tremendous obstacles that I had to overcome. I paid more, went into debt and abandoned a business. Because of some hasty decisions, I missed out on money-making opportunities and spent money on things that didn't work. I used so many heartbeats that did not lead me where I was trying to go.

Those poor decision in the early days of my ministry cost but the lessons were priceless. If you want to make your business and your ministry work, follow the treasure map in the scriptures to advance in the right direction. Make smart decisions and know when it's time to turn a corner and when to hold on and build your capacity.

You will make mistakes; we all do. But that's okay. The greatest teachable moments come through the mistakes we experience. They may start off as detours but when you keep pressing, your detours become your greatest steppingstones.

Reflections for my Wild Friends

When you start this journey, there is no way to know what you will face as you advance. But no matter what happens, you have the assurance that God gave you the assignment and He will finish what He starts. Try to focus more on following Him and less on controlling all your outcomes. Give yourself grace and freedom.

Your freedom makes you different; embrace it. It's who you are. Follow the Word and don't allow anyone to put a restraint on you that God does not state in the Scriptures. He needs you the way you are, anchored in Him, ready for good works.

"Being confident of this very thing, that He who has begun a good work in your will complete it until the day of Jesus Christ." (Philippians 1:6)

Seven

ANTICIPATE - Connect Your Marketplace Ministry To Your Life

"If money wasn't an issue,
what would you do?"

The early part of my career was in a corporate environment. I was a second level manager overseeing a sales territory. I thought I would never need another job. The pay was good. They gave me a company car, I traveled to beautiful places, rode in limousines and stayed in luxury resorts. An expense account allowed me to live well while I was on a fast track to upper management. Everything was going well but when the lifestyle got quiet, it always felt like there was something missing. I looked for things to do that would make me feel better. I remodeled my apartment, updated my wardrobe and joined social organizations. Still, something was always missing. I prayed and asked God what was going on. How could I be so unhappy and have so much? When people asked, "What's the problem? All I could say was, "I am supposed to be helping people." I was good at making a profit for my company but could not help myself.

At a weeklong management training exercise, they paired me with another manager. During one of our sessions, they asked, "What would you do if you only had one year to live?" The other manager quickly responded, "I certainly would not be doing this!" Surprised that he seemed just as unfulfilled as me, I asked him, "What would you be doing?" He said, "I would find something that has more meaning." All I could say was, "Yes! You nailed it." Money didn't make it meaningful. Unfortunately, my session partner tragically died in an auto accident a few weeks later. He didn't have time to make a new decision but I still had time. Two weeks later, I quit my job.

For the first few months after I quit my job, I did nothing. I had saved a nice sum of money and was used to spending. So, I just kept spending money. I even took a trip to Las Vegas. After all, my job was so stressful, I needed the break. As the money faded, I quickly learned that it would not be as easy as I thought to get back on my feet. I knew there was a better place for me but I couldn't find a route that made sense. I didn't know what to do next. Eventually and after a lot of wasted time, I found a job with less pay, fewer benefits and no perks. I had to work to pay the bills that were piling up. It felt good to walk away from the old job. I just wish I would have planned my "what's next." It took years for me to recover from making an excellent decision at the wrong time.

The What's Next

Throughout the day, you make many choices. There are a lot of opportunities to say yes or no. You can choose to say something or watch it happen. Every day, you decide to get up, talk to people and live your day. You decide if you want to confront the rude person in the check-out line at the store or just ignore them. You decide to dedicate your life to your job, family, ministry and so much more. Every day you make choices that determines how you live. You even get to decide how to respond to things you can't control. Things like bad weather and company-wide decisions made by upper management are beyond your control. Still, you get to decide how to respond and how you allow it to affect you. Those choices have attachments called "What's next?" Think about the choices you make and ask yourself, "What comes next?"

If you confront the rude person in the check-out line, "What's next?"

If you are diligent in your job, "What's next?"

If you show care and support for your family, "What's next?"

If you dedicate your life to ministry, "What's next?"

In all these situations the "What's next?" can move you forward and bring positivity to your life or send you backwards, creating chaos, hurt feelings and financial worries.

As you make smart decisions, think about "What's next?" If the thing that comes next appeals to you, perhaps it's a good choice. If not, maybe you should reflect for a while and find a smarter solution.

I wish I knew to think about the "What's next?" before I quit my job. I heard about the "What's next?" from a former co-worker and now I use it to make smart decisions. Now, as I reflect, quitting my job was the right thing to do but I should have waited until it was the right time. I would have planned much better before I quit my job. Better preparation would have saved me a lot of money and valuable time. With hindsight, I should have saved more money, paid off my debt and spent some time on my knees asking God for guidance. When I started my corporate job, it was after an extensive time of prayer. That job was my blessing! When God revealed He had more for me, it didn't mean that I had a free ticket to walk away from a blessing without considering His timing. Yes, He has a plan. He also knows when and how He wants you to carry out His plan.

Fast forward over 20 years. Here's what I learned from quitting my job too soon. Hopefully, it will help you as you seek God's guidance and His timing before you quit your job.

Manage your spending

When you know you're going to quit your job, stop spending money and start paying off debt. If you are stuck with a lot of debt, it limits your choices. You might take the wrong position or tolerate a job you don't like because you have bills to pay. Get the debt under control and seek to live well beneath your financial ability so you will have enough money to carry you while you transition to a new job.

Manage the timing of your exit

If possible, quit your job *after* you find a new one or when you have enough financial surplus to carry you until you can replace the income. There are no promises until you sign a contract for a new job. If needed, endure your current job for a while. Pray for your current job and for your coworkers. Pray for God to help you move in his timing. Do whatever it takes to stay where you are until it's the right time to leave.

Start your new business before you quit your job

Before you leave your old job, set up the foundational components of your new career or business (website, social media, insurance, office and marketing supplies, business plan, etc.).

Make a plan

Before you quit the old job, have a plan in place. Even if you feel you need a break, plan your time. How will you eat, pay bills and buy gas? Having your plan already in place makes your transition easier.

Do not burn old bridges

Leave your job with a good name. You have probably made some good social connections and friends in your current job. Keep their contact information and leave with the option to get a referral from your manager. Take care of loose ends and train your replacement, if necessary. There may be a time in the future when knowing someone from your old job works to your advantage. If they broke the trust, do your best to mend broken relationships and maintain an excellent reputation as you exit.

Create cash flow

Quitting your job can bring uncertainty. If possible, create some cash flow to make sure you meet your basic needs. It is important to do what you enjoy but doing what you enjoy costs money. Look for money-making opportunities that leave you the time and flexibility you need for your marketplace ministry.

Be discreet

I know it is exciting when you are on your way to greener pastures. Usually, it works better when you do not talk too much about your new plans while you're still at your old job. Talking could be a distraction for you and your co-workers. Yes, it's exciting to move on but make sure the people with whom you share your plans are supportive and desire the best for you.

Boldly step out at the right time

If you have planned, prayed and prepared and believe it is time to quit your job, then step into your next season! Put on your faith and trust God to help you meet challenges.

Grow where you are

I know how it feels to dislike your job. It's not that you don't want to work, it's just the job or a person, the pay or how you feel when you do certain tasks. Sometimes it is just wrong.

After I graduated from college, I really needed to make money. I had a job but it was a full-time, low-paying, data entry position I took just to get by while I finished my last semester of college. For eight hours a day, I worked full-time, with no benefits and barely made enough to pay my rent and car note. I filled out application after application and went on countless interviews but no one would hire me. It was so frustrating that I stopped looking.

On the job, we had to sit at our desk, not talk and quietly enter data. We had a 1-hour lunch and two 15-minute breaks. I felt like I had a right to be a terrible employee because I didn't like the job that left me feeling so down and with so much lack. So, I became even more miserable. I blamed the job for my problems. It was their fault that I could barely pay my bills. It was because of them that I couldn't afford any social activities. I didn't know why I couldn't find another job; I just knew it was not my fault. I was so miserable I started coming to work late, talking most of the time and producing just enough work to get by. As a new follower of Christ, I was eager to get my life in order but nothing I tried seemed to work. So, I gave up; I just stopped trying.

The one light in the position was our freedom to wear headphones while we worked. I usually listened to music but one day I turned on the radio and found a man teaching a Bible study. His name was Chuck Swindoll. His teaching style was so clear and easy to follow that I started listening to him every day. He was teaching a Bible study from the Old Testament about Moses and the Israelites' journey through the wilderness. It resonated with me and my situation. It was comforting to know I wasn't alone in feeling stuck. I tuned in every day to hear about God dealing with His people. It was easy to see why they didn't get to their promised land in the time expected. Before that study, I didn't know it was so important to follow God and do what He says. I saw how much the Israelites were missing by not following God's guidance.

"Why wouldn't they listen?" I kept asking. God was trying to advance them but they kept doing their own thing. They kept ignoring God and forgetting what He did for them. How could they be so blind? Then suddenly, like a mirror crashing on my head, I got it! Wow! I wasn't listening either.

The first Bible verse I embraced was Colossians 3:23, *"Whatever you do, work heartily, as for the Lord and not for men."*

I didn't know that how I worked mattered that much to God. I really thought I was free to decide based on how I felt and how they treated me. But I was wrong. After several weeks, God unlocked the secret and revealed what was happening in my life. The job was not the problem, I was.

I stopped acting like I worked for the manager, who walked around the room like a sergeant waiting to swat the hands of the class talker. She was no longer the focus because I realized I worked for God, not her. I decided that how I felt about her management style should not determine how I worked. All I needed to do was show God how I work for Him.

The next day, I arrived early, jumped on my computer and started working. My mouth was quiet and I didn't say a word to anyone. All day, I worked, took a break, went to lunch and came back on time. Following the rules, I worked as fast as I could. At the end of the week, a friend who handled quality control said, "Be careful, they have flagged you for an audit. They believe you are doing something wrong because your production has tripled. You are putting out more work than anyone in the company and they say that amount of work is impossible." I smiled and said, "There is nothing wrong. I am just working." God continued to open my eyes and show me areas in myself that needed to improve.

A few weeks later I was quietly working and stopped to glance around the room. "Where is everybody?" I asked the quality control person who was walking around the room.

"Haven't you heard? They are quietly calling people to the office and laying them off. They are not letting them come back to the floor for their personal items until the end of the day."

"Wow, I didn't know the company was in trouble. Maybe I should gather my things so if they call me I'll be ready."

She responded, "You don't have anything to worry about. They can't lay you off because you produce so much work."

Realizing that God changed me through His Word, I sat comfortably in my chair and smiled. Some people might say, "Won't He do it!"

Here's what I learned from that experience. I hope it helps you too.

- I learned to work for God and seek to be extremely good at my work.

- I also learned to get over the belief that just because I graduated from college that I deserved a better job. That was not wrong but we all deserved better. A college degree creates more opportunities but it doesn't make us better than anyone else.
- I realized that no person or job should ever negatively influence you to the point of shaping your personality or making you step away from God's plan.
- I understood that we must find our peace, joy and happiness, even when parts of our lives are undesirable. My peace came while working on that job because I knew God was working on me. I still didn't like it but I didn't complain. I was grateful for the ability to work, get paid and pay my bills.

After I put these steps in action, everything changed. I got a call. "Hey, Rhonda, are you still looking for a job?" I replied, Yes! I got a job that I really wanted and my life transformed on the outside just like it transformed on the inside!

There will always be less favorable aspects to getting the job done. However, when you focus on God's plan instead of yours, it feels good to know that He works through you. He is always doing more than you think. Early in my career, I didn't understand this principle. My decisions were based on what I wanted and how I felt. I didn't look at how my decisions affected other people. Now I know the decisions I make connect to people and events, now and in the future. It's not just about what you want and don't want. We all must think about the cost and timing of our decisions and how we influence others. There are also substantial rewards for diligently working. It may not seem like it, but God uses work to teach us valuable lessons that we can't learn any other way.

Be willing to learn and grow

Before you decide to quit your job, pray and see if God is trying to teach you something at your current job. Sometimes God allows you to stay in a tough situation to help you grow and qualify for your future place. If you bail out too soon, He will bring you back to the same place to try again. He will let you stay in that place until you learn the lesson. Why? Because He is eager for you to get to the treasure on His map.

Even with this information, I know people who still believe they should quit their job. My goal is not to tell you what to do, but to encourage you to reflect and make a careful decision. If God says, "It's time to leave," go! If He says, "Wait," wait! If He says, "No," stay!

Consider a side-hustle

It is hard to work on a job that you don't like. Sometimes God instructs you to move and sometimes He wants you to stay; both decisions require growth. You grow when you stay on a job that you don't like and you also grow when you step out by faith and start something new. One middle ground is to move from the old job but find a side-hustle to sustain you while you transition. Some side hustles are so lucrative that you need nothing else.

As companies downsize, limit benefits and automate, the idea of loyalty extending to longevity is fading. It is becoming more difficult for people to stay on jobs that give them little satisfaction and purpose. Of course, there are many reasons to stay on a job but sometimes you still can't stay. If that sounds like you and you don't have the money you need, consider a side-hustle. Choosing a side hustle is the bridge for many people to keep the bills paid. According to the 2019 United States Census Bureau, over 13 million United States workers have more than one job. Some side-hustles become so lucrative they turn into full-time jobs or businesses. It's nice to know you have options.

For example, working for Door Dash, Uber, Lyft, Instacart or one of the other ride-sharing companies is an easy way to make quick money for groceries, to pay a few bills or get some spending money. There are also excellent options in multi-level marketing but be careful of organizations that have large payments to start and pressure you to recruit your family and friends. In most cities in the U.S., there are ways to make extra cash if you are willing to do the work. Before you decide, think about these questions.

- How much upfront money do you need?
- How long does it take to make money?
- Will you need to make cold calls?
- Do you need a license or certification?
- Can you get residual income?
- Do you like the people and the service or product?
- How is their training?
- Do they have an excellent reputation?
- Where will you find your customers?
- Is your personality right for this business?

The extra income is a good way to bridge financial gaps and make sure your basic needs are met. It also gives you time to reflect on your business and ministry goals. If your goal is to make money so you can be free to quit your job and enjoy other activities, don't accept a side hustle that can't get you to your goal. Career changes happen. The only way to step up is to step out of the old and into the new. When you are ready, just make sure you do it the right way.

Did you know God instructed us to work? In the Bible, Adam and Eve had work to do.

"Then the Lord God formed man of dust from the ground and breathed into his nostrils the breath of life; and man became a living being. The Lord God planted a garden toward the east, in Eden; and there he placed the man whom he had formed. Out of the ground the Lord God caused to grow every tree that is pleasing to the sight and good for food; the tree of life also in the midst of the garden, and the tree of the knowledge of good and evil....Then the Lord God took the man and put him into the garden of Eden to cultivate it and keep it." (Genesis 2:7-9;15)

A few years ago, I had this cool idea to start a garden in my backyard. My husband dug up a small space with enough room to grow just enough organic veggies for our family and a few friends. The space was perfect but the soil needed work. So, I added more soil and some fertilizer alone with twelve plants. It was not long before the weeds started taking over. Every morning when I checked my garden my vegetables grew and the weeds grew. I pulled weeds almost every day. One day, I went outside, expecting to pull a few weeds and harvest a few vegetables but something was wrong. I found holes in the leaves of my plants. What was happening? The worms were having a good time eating my plants! I didn't want to use a harsh chemical on my food, so I found a safe treatment for my problem. I love my garden but it's hard work! It would have been easy to spray a chemical on the worms but my organic garden would suffer. Although it takes time to manage a garden and find the right products, I enjoy my garden. I understand there is no easy way to do it right. But when I see my family enjoying a salad with the vegetables that I picked from the garden, I remember why I do it. I remember that nothing worthwhile comes easy. After all, it is called work.

As you think and reflect on your job, business and marketplace ministry, understand that it won't be easy but the work has glorious rewards. There is not a mistake that is too big or difficult for God to help you recover. You can leave, stay, get a side-hustle or make a change on the same job. Whatever you choose, be sure to give God your best and be open to His timing and direction. Remember to always consider the "What's next?"

Reflections for my Wild Friends

When you decide to be anchored in Jesus Christ and work for Him with His plan, don't allow worry to bombard you. God is so excited to have you loving Him, that He will make sure His will works in you. He has already invested heavily in your well-being and He is not about to stop. Invest in quietness regularly and listen for His guidance. Study the Scriptures and listen to only wise counsel. When you work hard and put His Word ahead of your desires, He will get you where He wants you.

"The steps of a good man are ordered by the Lord, And He delights in his way. Though he fall, he shall not be utterly cast down; For the Lord upholds him with His hand." (Psalm 37:23-24)

3

UNLEASH YOUR WILD CAPACITY

Eight

BUILD AND MULTIPLY - Manage Your Money and Your Motives

"There is limited value in pressing, growing and making money if it doesn't help others. Life is always about more than just you."

When you talk about money, it doesn't take long to find an opinion.

Prosperity leaders say, "You deserve to be rich." People who take a vow of poverty say, "You're blessed to be poor."

A business owner says, "It's all about profit."

A pastor says, "It's all about people."

While everyone has an opinion, you reveal your belief about money by how you manage what you have. However, the truth about money is in the Scriptures, which makes all the opinions and traditions take a backseat.

You don't need money to do ministry. Ministry happens when you help, assist, serve, worship and use your spiritual gifts in a manner that glorifies God. Ministry is work but it's meaningful and it helps people. In marketplace ministry, we help people but we also point them to God's love and His Word. Ministry in this form does not require money. That's why you don't have to delay your ministry. You can pray for people and show God's love anytime and anywhere. If you say you can't minister or use your spiritual gifts because you don't have money or a place to function, what message does that send to people who live in remote places around the world and don't have the money-making opportunities that some people enjoy? Are they unable to minister? Of course, they can. If you can't have a ministry without money, what message does that send to a grandmother with limited resources but a heart for God that is deep and wide? While money is a great tool that provides many opportunities and choices, it does not determine your calling or the depth of God's ability to use you. God blesses people with and without money.

Operating a ministry is a different story. Ministry operations may include a physical location, repairs, equipment and the daily needs to keep the ministry functioning. The person who handles payroll and the person who creates professional, well-branded marketing material will probably want to get paid. You'll need a paid professional to get good content for your website and social media sites. There are countless other supplies that your ministry needs, like office and meeting space, furniture, computers, printers and apps, all requiring money. Yes, you may find volunteers to handle some jobs but as you build and multiply, your payroll needs will increase too.

In business, executives go through extreme measures to reach their financial goals. They do it for the sake of the business, profits, status and power. In ministry, we too should give all we have to reach our financial goals, except we do it for God's glory to further His kingdom, not our own. You can't be passive about managing money when it influences how well your ministry operates and the extent that you accomplish your ministry goals. A proper perspective about money requires you to be a good steward of what God gives you. It positions you to honor God as you make and manage money.

To build and multiply takes money. As you make the money you need, your motives are even more important. When you don't have the money to make foolish financial decisions, it protects you from allowing foolish financial decisions to hurt your market ministry. Nonetheless, when you have money, you also have increased options. Those increased options give you a feeling of freedom that can be intoxicating if not bridled. In marketplace ministry, your Statement of Faith and your ministry statements will help you manage your motives and stay on the right course.

Three Money Rules for Your Marketplace Ministry

Manage Your Income

Optimize your money-making ability and multiply your financial opportunities. Money is a means for exchange and gives you an array of choices. If God gives you the opportunity to make money, He has a purpose for the money that you receive (Matthew 25: 14-30).

Manage Your Motives

Love God and love others but don't love your money. There is nothing evil about having and enjoying your money. However, it is very easy for your heart to change when money is plentiful. Be careful not to love your money (making it first in your heart above everything else), which opens doors to all manner of evil (1 Timothy 6:10).

Manage Your Giving

The best deterrent from the love of money is giving. The freedom to make money is a blessing and a privilege. When you make it, you have a responsibility to give cheerfully (2 Corinthians 9: 6-7). Giving takes your eyes off yourself and reminds you of the needs of others.

Perspectives about managing money start long before you have money to manage. It starts when you see a parent handling money. You learn from conversations around the table. You learn it when you have a traumatic hurtful event involving a lack of money. For example, being the only child in class who wears a low-cost brand of shoes or used, outdated clothes. If you have ever been hungry with no food, that traumatic experience shapes you. Your childhood experiences shape what you believe. If you grow up with plenty, it influences you differently than a person who grows up experiencing lack. You can also become entitled and believe you deserve wealth when you get too much with no responsibility.

These experiences create spaces in your mind that influence your money decisions as an adult. The good news is that you can learn positive money management skills. If you don't like your money situation, change it. Learn new behavior and change your life. Your marketplace ministry needs you to manage your money, motives and giving. Anyone who believes that making money doesn't matter is not considering the big picture. Money is not just for you. It is supposed to go through you to benefit others. You are blessed to be a blessing!

I have observed people who have plenty of money and those who consistently lack enough money. I have also experienced both sides of the coin. Some people, I call them money magnets, consistently make and keep money. They always seem to land on the positive side of cash flow. It may look like luck but it's not that simple. Money does not come through magic. When you see a financially successful magnet, they are operating with habits, behaviors, expectations and principles that work overtime. Everything that works for them can also work for you. It happens when you sift through your habits and allow growth and learn through change. Then over time, you develop a pattern of success and your confidence increases. Your new confidence attracts others, which open doors and opportunities for success. The difference between a person who multiplies and grows a marketplace ministry and a normal money magnet is motives. Marketplace ministry leaders build and multiply with a motive to honor God in business and ministry. Magnets build with no view of God's desires. They build for themselves.

Since you are called to marketplace ministry, you are already a step ahead of most people. Marketplace ministry leaders have spiritual gifts and talents that are useful in business and ministry. Yes, that's right, my wild friend! God gave you an extra dose of ability in both areas. Don't ignore your talents. If you know how to make money, go for it! Think about all that you can change when you have the financial ability to solve problems and make a difference in the life of people and organizations. Go forward with everything you have, then build on it and multiply.

In Chapter 7, I mentioned a one-week training I attended that involved an intense personality assessment. That course helped me understand how I relate to people in business and how people perceive me. I completed a long questionnaire with details about my preferences and beliefs. The course facilitator reviewed my profile results and said, "Interesting. I rarely find someone whose results are so evenly divided." My profile showed two main areas of strength that were almost 50/50, while most people had one clear dominate area and a few secondary areas, I showed an even interest in business and service. She explained that it would not satisfy me to have one career. If I pursued business, I would feel like something was missing. If I switched to ministry or service, I would still feel incomplete. The only solution was to do both. Wow! That is marketplace ministry to the core.

Wild friends, I don't know what your score would be but I know if you feel drawn to both ministry and business, that means God wired you that way. Embrace your call and let's get it done!

There is nothing wrong with enjoying a beautiful home, designer clothes, and many of life's delicacies. That's called enjoying life. Just make sure that's not all that you care about. Make sure material gain is not your top priority because it will never really satisfy you. The more you pursue God's agenda, the less significant material gain becomes. I am not saying you won't enjoy nice things; but you won't wrap your identity in your possessions. Instead, you become excited about stepping into your true identity in Christ, which is a priceless possession that money can't buy.

Watch out for sidesteps

Once you decide to build and multiply, it's common to get offers that lure you away from what God is doing. I believe these offers threaten your marketplace ministry. They are subtle but fierce. I call them sidesteps. A sidestep is a decision that is slightly off track but seems innocent. It pretends to solve a problem or add an extra dimension to your goals. However, as time passes, it yields bitter fruit and seeks to get you so off track it's difficult to recover. A sidestep seems harmless. You think it means nothing, so you agree. All the time, it chips away your momentum, ultimately delaying your progress and stifling your growth.

To protect yourself, identify your non-negotiables. No matter how much money you need or how much you make, make some baseline commitments that you won't change. Also, revisit the 8 Principles of a Marketplace Ministry in Chapter 4.

Here are a few examples:

- God always comes first
- Your family is your top priority
- You will be honest and above reproach
- You will be a good steward with money
- You will be a giver
- You will use your gifts for God
- You will seek to live according to the Scriptures
- You will cherish your personal relationship with Jesus Christ and seek to know Him better

How to recognize a sidestep

To recognize a sidestep, pay attention to opportunities and ideas that are close to your non-negotiables but are just a little off. Sirens should go off when you hear something like:

"You are overreacting. It's okay to make this decision to stop giving so much. That's just business."

"I know you wanted to go to your son's baseball game on Thursdays but attending this program on Thursdays is very important. It can take your business to a new level. That's what you want, right?"

"You are being too nice to your team. They might forget that you're the boss."

"Why do you take the time to call people to congratulate them? Can't you get someone to send a card?"

"I know this investment has nothing to do with ministry or your business but so many people are making money. You don't want to pass this up."

Do you see it? There is nothing wrong with the statements except they are all a sidestep from your commitment. We must filter every important decision through God's Word before we agree, comment or make a move. The reason this is so important for marketplace ministry is because you operate in a business culture that does not consider the Bible as a leadership source. The business world doesn't see many successful, influential followers of Christ. Going against the norm takes intentional effort and a willingness to be different, even when it's not popular. We will talk more about it and how to fight it in Chapter 10.

The road that most people take is wide and easy when they simply follow everyone else; it's easy to just fit in. However, the marketplace ministry road is narrow. It has obstacles designed to take you away from your ministry goals, so you will not magnify God. Think about it. How many ways do you see God being magnified in the business world? Yes, He gets His glory but what a privilege to be a part of God's work in the business world and in your community.

Here are some non-negotiable commitments that will help you stay on track.

- Have a commitment to excel in business and ministry
- Create a loving culture in your business and ministry
- Embrace your freedom to honor God at work
- Be intentional about developing opportunities for others
- Have authentic care for business associates and their concerns
- Encourage spiritual and personal growth for all team members
- Encourage everyone to make money, be a good steward and use their resources to help others
- Foster balance and an enjoyment of life and work

Identifying obstacles

Unlike sidesteps, which are decisions you make, you will also encounter obstacles, which are positions that block your progress. When you commit to being a Christ-follower, you will have obstacles designed to stop your progress. These obstacles are in plain sight, standing in your way, slowly eroding your ministry plans.

Obstacles often come as people who don't understand your marketplace ministry goals. The results are the same despite the different ways they operate. These subtle messages discourage you with negativity and gossip. You hear statements designed to make you question your decisions. They make suggestions that block your progress seek to shift you in a different direction. Obstacles come as spiritual warfare (more on this subject in Chapter 10) where odd events happen like technology issues, people problems and delayed approvals. Yes, when you set out to honor God with your money and your business, you attract all kinds of resistance. While obstacles will come, trust God, who called you on this journey. Whatever He calls you to, He will see you through.

Obstacles even come as confusion and poor advice, seeking to bring feelings of uncertainty.

"I think you should change your business model."
"I think you should work with a different group of people."
"I think you should add something and remove something."
"I think you should lighten up."

People love to help you be like them. Well-meaning advice is not always good advice. When considering advice from others, ask yourself:

Does this person genuinely care about me and what God is doing in my life?

Does the person have a proven track record? Are they qualified to give good advice based on their own successful experiences?

When you step into a new opportunity, it's easy to be sidetracked. The more people you allow to get into your mind, the more likely you are to experience unwanted hinderances. This is important, because when you step into a new venture, your old thinking and old habits are comfortable with the old way. Familiarity feels more comfortable, so it is easy to justify decisions that are familiar but wrong. That's when familiarity is your enemy and leads to self-sabotage. No one needs to stop you because you stop yourself.

How to overcome sidesteps and obstacles

When you are delayed by sidesteps and obstacles, be patient and give yourself time to recover. It takes time to reframe your thoughts and create new actions. Start by learning Bible verses that address what you are experiencing. Meditate on the passages daily and let the truth sink into your heart and mind. Also, place yourself in new environments where people live and think differently from you. Look for conversations to join, places to go and new friends to hang with. Then observe, listen and learn. No matter what tries to stop you, gather yourself and your commitment to having a thriving marketplace ministry. Above all, hold tight to biblical truths.

Building and multiplying in your community

God blesses us, not just for us to enjoy but for us to extend the blessing to others. Life is always about more than just you. There is limited value in pressing, growing and making money if it doesn't help others. Your community needs you; people need your gifts. They need to see you being successful and caring about your community. When people see your success, it gives the people hope and belief that they can do it too. People also benefit from your talent and giving. I like the quote, "Money doesn't solve all your problems but it gives you more options."

How often have you seen a follower of Christ with money to influence people, environments and situations? As marketplace ministry leaders, we are the ones who are called to use our gifts and make a difference in the lives of others. This can happen through the people that you hire. It may happen through your testimony about Christ. It may be as simple as paying for dinner for a group of people. Sometimes, a great tip and a message, "God loves you," opens the heart of a server. You will find opportunities to give to your local schools, summer camps and the less fortunate. Financial resources not only change your life but from the heart of a cheerful giver, it changes the life of others too.

Building and multiplying requires you to attract people and care for the people that you attract. It's great to have a business idea. It's even better to know how to find the people who will pay for what you are offering. Being a great salesperson with a wonderful product will get you in the door but it won't get you a seat at the table with key players and an invitation to come again. The goal is to attract people and create an active style with so much momentum that new doors open and new opportunities arise.

Look for ways to brand yourself with your creativity and your genuine care for your customers or clients. People know you are offering a product or service but they still want you to be authentic and show that you care. Being authentic means listening and being honest. People need to know that they can trust you. They appreciate listeners who don't always have to tell their own story. It's okay to hold back on talking about yourself so you can listen carefully to someone else. That's what building relationships is all about. Consciously decide not to dominate the conversation talking about yourself. Listen. Ask questions. Show people that they matter.

The Sower

Take a moment and read Matthew 25: 14-30. Jesus uses a parable (a story to illustrate a point) to show how He feels about making a profit. In this Parable of the Talents, a master went away and trusted his money with three people. When he returned, he expected to receive a profit. He gave each person a different amount of money based on ability. In the end, to the ones who earned a profit, he gave more. The one who did nothing lost what he had.

When you have money, God expects you to manage it well and multiply what we have. If we are passive, we lose what we have.

2 Corinthians 9:6-8 tells us:

"Now this I say, he who sows sparingly will also reap sparingly, and he who sows bountifully will also reap bountifully. Each one must do just as he has purposed in his heart, not grudgingly or under compulsion, for God loves a cheerful giver. And God is able to make all grace abound to you,

so that always having all sufficiency in everything, you may have an abundance for every good deed."

Obviously, God cares about how you make money and what you do with the money you receive. So, let's put it all together.

- Work diligently, no matter how much money you make. Diligent work brings rewards (Proverbs 12:24).
- Be content when money is flowing well and be content when money is tight (1 Timothy 6:6-12).
- Never be a lover of money (1 Timothy 6:10).
- Be smart about managing your money and multiply what you have (Proverbs 21:20).
- Be a giver (2 Corinthians 9:6-7).
- Build and multiply your marketplace ministry vision (Matthew 25: 14-30).

Check out how the Matthew parable ends.

"For to everyone who has, more will be given, and he will have an abundance. But from the one who does not have, even what he has will be taken away from him." (Matt 25:29)

Are you losing money because of how poorly you manage what you have?

Are you missing a blessing or God's favor because you aren't passionate about what you do? Want to find favor in business and ministry? Work like God is your supervisor.

Are you using half of what He has given you or bringing it all to the table?

Colossians 3:23 says, *"Whatever you do, work heartily, as for the Lord and not for men."* That includes your business.

Here's the good news (Proverbs 22:19) *"Do you see a man skillful in his work? He will stand before kings; he will not stand before obscure men."*

Wild friends, do you see the connection? Take what you have, build it, multiply it, honor God and see Him bless you with more. This is a business and spiritual principle that cannot fail.

Reflections for my Wild Friends

As I said earlier, money is a big deal. It is one of the big three; money, power and sex. That's why you must assess your motives regularly. I have seen many otherwise trustworthy people flip when money became plentiful. The enjoyment of the options that money provides can intoxicate you. That's why giving is so important because it takes the focus off you.

As you become successful, keep yourself humble and accountable. Don't take a stage just because people will give you a pedestal. Take the stage that's right for you. Money is not evil. It is a means of exchange. But the love of money is the problem. The Bible says it is the root of all kinds of evil. When you see a problem or have a question about an issue, always seek God's guidance. Then, learn to follow the money. You will often find a path that clarifies where people stand.

Protect yourself by being above reproach. If a decision places your integrity in question, stay away. Yes, make your money. But see it for what it's worth. It does not define you. It just helps you get where you are trying to go and hopefully, enjoy the journey.

Nine

PRESS AND MOVE - Finish What You Start

"The starting line is crowded with people who are dreamers. The finish line is sparse with people who are finishers."

The average worker spends more hours working, preparing for work and going to work, than any other activity. When you spend that much time on an activity, you need to make it count. You can be certain that God sees you. Don't lock Him in the corridors of a religious institution. Jesus is an engaging companion who goes where you go. He goes to your business and anywhere else He chooses. Whatever you do at work and in business, look around, He is in the room. God cares what's happening in your business and He cares about how you treat people. He cares what you do with your money and He expects you to press in and make significant strides in your ministry and business.

Working is an expectation from God. Genesis 2:15 says, *"The Lord God took the man and put him in the garden of Eden to work it and keep it."* The same applies today. Your garden is where you have authority, where you live, go to church, hang out and get paid. Your marketplace ministry is a part of your garden but as I mentioned earlier, it takes work to cultivate a garden.

Reflect on the goals and statements that you wrote in Chapters 4, 5 and 6 of this book. Take some time to pray about your goals and ask God,

"How can I press into these goals?"

"Have I limited myself in any way?"

"Is there anything that I did not consider that you want me to do?"

"Have I allowed my past to dictate my future negatively?"

"Am I blocking your direction? Am I listening well?"

God is always doing more than you think. If you ask these questions and nothing changes, move forward but keep your heart open for change. As you move forward, understand that change happens. There is no easy way to build and multiply without pressing in.

You press when you don't have the help you need and when you have a personal challenge. Life gives you many reasons to stop pursuing a marketplace ministry. Sometimes the only way to keep going is to press in.

There is something special about people who presses in, perseveres through trials and refuses to give up. They keep adjusting, keep learning and keep pushing until they create a momentum that eventually moves in their favor. Faith and work go together and steadfastness leads to blessing. Most things that are worthwhile aren't easy to get, like diamonds and pearls. Don't settle for the easy goals. Instead, go for the prize and get the blessing. When it gets tough, consider that God always has a plan. He knows the beginning and the end. You may not know what He is doing but He will bless you when you press in and trust Him. Trusting in this way means putting your ways aside and applying His will and His Word to your situation. In this place, you can't lose because you are actively involved in God's business, not just standing on the sidelines watching other people live.

Don't get caught up watching other people live when you don't know their actual story or their back story. You don't know who has prayed for them. They could live in the spotlight of their parents' and grandparents' prayers. You don't know God's plan and purpose for them and others involved. What God does in another person's life is between them and God, just like your relationship is between you and God.

Remember, everything that looks good is not a blessing. Instead, as you walk through this journey, have a heart of praise, make peace when possible and always seek God for direction. Your press in is for your blessing. Don't compare yourself to anyone because your journey is unlike anyone else's journey. Allow God to guide you as you press in and He directs your steps. Trust God and His work in you and in your situation.

Press in with preparation

If you press and pray for God to elevate you, stay ready. You never know when God will send a great opportunity your way. Sometimes you believe all you need is one more step when God is looking for six steps. You think you're not ready when God says, "Today is your day." His ways are not our ways and His thoughts are not ours (Isaiah 55: 8-9). If you are pressing in and waiting on God, spend the time learning to understand what God wants. When you understand where He's leading, your press in becomes fortified.

Here are a few stories of how God can bless you and why it's important to be ready.

Example #1 - Praying for the money to further his education

A person was praying and fasting for God to provide a way to pay for college tuition. While enjoying a sporting event, she heard a conversation that sparked her interest. As the crowd calmed down, she heard a woman next to her talking to her friend, "I still don't have my recommendations for the college fund. I need 3 more names by tomorrow but I can't find enough people who qualify."

Would you be able to introduce yourself in a way that positions you for the scholarship? Do you already have the grades, community service hours and some good character recommendations? If not, perhaps God is not answering the prayer today because you are not ready today. Instead of just praying for God to bless you, pray and ask Him how you should press in to be ready when the right opportunity comes.

Example #2 - Praying for God to give you a larger platform

What if you were a dancer seeking a larger stage to showcase your talent and advance your dancing career? As you are enjoying dinner with friends, you hear a man at the table say, "Our last audition for the National Dance Team is tomorrow but I'm really not satisfied with the candidates." Would you be ready to ask for the opportunity to audition? Would you be ready for an audition tomorrow? Do you have your resume complete? Are you in shape for a rigorous schedule? Are you ready for God to answer your prayer?

God doesn't want you to wait until he blesses you to get ready. He wants you prepared *before* He makes a move. That gets you ready, not only for the benefits of your promotion but also for the responsibility and the challenges that every promotion brings.

Here are a few more ways to be ready for God to elevate you:

Be ready by practicing your elevator pitch. This is a brief description about you that sells your skills. Learn to explain who you are and what you offer to a person on an elevator ride if needed.

Be ready to deliver your talent with passion. God gave you gifts and talents and He wants the greatest return on what He gives. Remember Matthew 25:14-30?

Be ready with the right credentials and experience. Fortunately, God has given us all that we need in the Scriptures to study and enjoy a vibrant relationship with Him (a formal study program is still very beneficial). However, in the culture, you need to compete with other standards that require additional education. Get what you need to become an expert in your field.

Press in, keep learning and getting better at your skill. Allow minor victories to prepare you for a greater future. It may take longer than you planned, but the wait is a perfect opportunity to be ready when God is ready. Don't wait to get ready. Be ready now! *Life favors the prepared and if you are prepared, life will favor you!*

Press into a closer relationship with Jesus Christ

God loves to spend time with you. You can experience God by embarking on a day-by-day journey to know Him and what He says about your life. Even if you have questions and situations that you don't understand, still seek Him, study His Word and do what it says.

"Blessed is the man who walks not in the counsel of the wicked, nor stands in the way of sinners, nor sits in the seat of scoffers; but his delight

is in the law of the Lord, and on his law, he meditates day and night. He is like a tree planted by streams of water that yields its fruit in its season, and its leaf does not wither. In all that he does, he prospers." (Psalm 1:1-3)

When you have a proven track record in business and you serve God, that takes you to a new level of influence. It's a recipe to attract more people to your faith and the opportunity to build your business with favor. God is not sitting back as you live and build your marketplace ministry. He wants to be involved in your personal and business life. God guides and directs you far beyond your plans or thoughts. He wants a close relationship with you in everything that you do. A direct result of your relationship with Jesus is prayer. It is a necessary part of your daily routine and should be included as a part of your scheduled daily routine and activities.

Press in with praise and worship

Music touches the soul and authentic worship touches God. No matter what is happening, try to put everything aside and spend some time worshipping God daily. Get focused by reading a scripture passage that honors God, then sing right where you are, in a group or alone. You can sing a song that you know or make up a song. Just tell God how amazing He is. Tell Him you love him. Then think about what He has done for you and tell him thank you!

Press in by sharing your faith with others

In marketplace ministry, we minister to others because of our love for Christ. It doesn't matter if people believe in our faith or not. Our ministry does not focus on what people do but on what Jesus Christ has already done.

Freely share conversations about your faith. If they are interested, gladly invite them to enjoy your resources like Bible Study.

Ephesians 3:20-21 says:

"Now to Him who is able to do far more abundantly beyond all that we ask or think, according to the power that works within us, to Him be the glory in the church and in Christ Jesus to all generations forever and ever. Amen."

Finish What You Start

I love to hear people share the exceptional things God is laying on their heart. There are books for you to write, youth ministries waiting to start and music waiting to be played. Yes! There are people ready to witness God's life-changing work through you. It's important to press, advance, align and plan. Beginning doesn't matter if you don't finish what you start.

There are so many reasons to start and not finish. Personal issues happen. Family problems occur. When you start a marketplace ministry, things will change but the mission must continue. That means you become the personal CEO of your life. You're not just a fan of ministry and business. Instead, you are fully immersed. The sideline is not the stop for you, because you want to be in the game leading and strategizing. You are the CEO for your marketplace ministry and a key player who cares for yourself so you can finish what you start.

When your personal CEO is in the right place, you create systems, routines and habits that lead to your success. You don't just start; you finish! Why? because you see your business as a ministry, not just a personal desire to earn income. Without your personal CEO, emotional challenges will derail your marketplace ministry and familiar habits will distract you. When you embrace your personal CEO, accomplishing your goals is not just based on feelings but a deep commitment to fulfill a call.

Your personal CEO influences every area of life. Answer these questions and think about how effective your personal CEO manages your goals.

Are you leading life or just responding to what happens to you?

Do you set goals and create routines to accomplish them or set the goal and walk away?

Do you stay on task even when you get resistance or turn away when it gets hard?

The signs of how your CEO manages your life will show in your finances, relationships and the people you hang with.

You decide when to wake up.

You decide to stay on task.

You decide to allow or ignore distractions.

You decide to join negative conversations or find a positive outlook.

You decide to be happy about a new day.

You decide to bring your "A" game.

You decide not to complain even when you have a reason.

You decide to follow the path that pleases God.

You decide to bring passion and diligence to the management of your life.

You decide to learn, build and grow.

Even if you feel that your life is spiraling out of control, you get to decide how to respond to what's happening. You decide to pray, seek help, cry and get back up.

You can manage your life well or manage it poorly. You are the CEO of your thoughts and your actions. Even God, in His sovereignty, gives you free will.

"For you were called to freedom, brethren; only do not turn your freedom into an opportunity for the flesh, but through love serve one another." (Galatians 5:13)

In a business, the CEO is the highest-ranking executive who makes major decisions and manages the operations and resources of a company. In your life, you are the highest-ranking person (apart from God). You manage your resources and your daily operations. You decide how to respond to every opportunity that comes your way.

Yes, God is in control, but He gives you responsibility, too. What choices do you have? Here are a few ideas:

You can go back to something that you started and decide that nothing will stop you.

You can change your attitude.

You can find new strength and ignore the crazy stuff.

You can work harder to find the solutions that you need.

You can pray. Then pray harder.

You can find Bible verses that help you grow.

You can ask for help.

You can forgive yourself (and others).

You can lock arms and share life with someone and grow together.

You can study business and ministry and learn what you need to move forward.

The point is to do something that leads you toward your goals and the finish line. You need your personal CEO to get beyond your emotions, people, disappointments and experiences so you can finish what you start. Be "all in" even when you don't have all the answers. What you have is the opportunity to move forward today, even if it's a small step.

Manage your personal CEO and finish what you start, so you will qualify for the next level. Whatever you do, don't stop. CEOs never stop growing and learning. They are change agents. Embrace your personal CEO and be patient with yourself.

It is challenging to go hard in your business and ministry and be "all in," yet gentle and caring for people in the marketplace. People have needs that take time and have nothing to do with your business goals. When you're "all in" to draw people toward Christ, you don't have time for detours and time wasters. Here are some issues to watch out for.

Petty arguments
Shallow conversations
Foolish distractions
Busyness with the wrong projects
Feeling sorry for yourself
Negative thoughts
Meaningless meetings
Listening to people who ramble and complain
Giving your power to other people
Blaming people when things go wrong

A Balanced Life

When a people arrive at a good place in their business and ministry but lose their family, they miss the genuine joy of the victory. Success comes and goes but your relationships with your family and other important people are lasting and generational. The most cherished memories always involve time you share with people.

The greatest satisfaction comes as you relate to people and enjoy meaningful relationships. Your greatest value and contribution to the world directly relates to the difference you make in the lives of others.

Don't give up your people-loving side to pursue your money-making goals. That will ultimately leave you empty and unfulfilled.

Remember, money gives you options but it doesn't give you joy and peace.

Instead, learn to balance your love for people and your passion to go hard in your business and ministry. Decide what's important and always carve out some time for people. Then be all in with them when you are together. Also, allocate some time each week to get quiet and think about how you're doing on the people-loving side.

Listen to people who tell you the truth, even if you don't like it. They will tell you if they feel neglected.

Give people open opportunities to discuss how they feel.

Have fun outside of work.

Don't take yourself you seriously. Laugh. Play. Be nice.

New business opportunities come and go. People, however, are a more important, lasting and a valuable part of your big picture and your overall enjoyment of life.

Don't just start. Finish!

Reflections for my Wild Friends

I know a lot of gifted and talented wild friends. They often share their dreams and the awesome call of God on their life. I see people get started, dreaming of conquering the vision that's in their heart. It's easy to talk about but it takes courage to take the first step. Starting is a great accomplishment but finishing is a much greater success!

When you step into this call, expect God to lead you on a journey that will deliver much more that you think. Through this process, He will refine you, make you bolder and strip you of hindering habits and people.

God doesn't operate with one generational goal. His picture is much bigger. No matter what happens, stay the course. If you don't understand, keep going. When you get disappointed, don't stop. Eventually, the surrounding events will no longer be a threat because you just won't stop! No matter what happens, stopping is not an option. When you get to this place, look for God to make a move.

Ten

STAND - Position Yourself For Victory

"Standing on God's Word is Your Greatest Weapon."

Mighty warriors have graced the pages of best-selling books and captured our attention on the big screen. They expand the imagination of starry-eyed children and fun-living adults around the world. Adorned with elaborate costumes and statuesque physiques, these warriors defy human boundaries and stand in the adversary's face, courageously fighting their battles until the enemy falls. They are heroes, protectors, kings, queens and noble knights in shining armor who defy their enemy to take a stand. These superheroes fight for their country and the universe. They fight for their family and for freedom. They fight for love and everything that's dear to them. But there's one thing that the mighty warrior on the pages or the screen never fights for, that's you and me!

I enjoy watching Captain America boldly stand for justice with a force that few can withstand. The well-written Avengers movies gathered heroes from other worlds to protect the earth from self-proclaimed gods seeking to conquer and destroy. As of June 2019, over 182 million people watched the Avengers movie, breaking several box office records since its $300 million debut (marvel.com).

Wow! We love our mighty warriors on screen. However, being entertained by them means sitting and engulfing ourselves into a great story about someone else. We give our precious heartbeats to watch a story created by a group of people, most likely doing what they enjoy. There is nothing wrong with enjoying a good fight in a top-rated movie but make sure they are not the only ones willing to fight for what they believe. Your fight is real and you also must stand against your adversary.

You may not be in the movies or on a physical battlefield but moving forward in your marketplace ministry still brings opposition. Your victory highly depends on your ability to discover and unleash your personal warrior.

I wish I could tell you that once you answer the call to marketplace ministry that it's going to be smooth sailing but I can't. What I can tell you is that you are about to embark on a journey that will take you places that you never thought of going. You will grow in ways that you never thought of growing and you will have no regrets for a well-fought battle.

This is the part where you adjust your mindset and decide to get into the game. Your passion and commitment to have your own marketplace ministry is now running the show to fulfill your dreams and possess God's treasure. A marketplace ministry is bigger than you because it extends beyond your heartbeats and into glory. When you fight a good fight and finish strong, after your last breath on earth, you will stand alive in the presence of Jesus Christ and hear him say, "Well done my good and faithful servant." (Matthew 25:21) That is the treasure!

Now that we have established the right mindset, let's talk about how to position yourself for victory and withstand the forces that will try to stop you.

"For our struggle is not against flesh and blood, but against the rulers, against the powers, against the world forces of this darkness, against the spiritual forces of wickedness in the heavenly places." (Ephesians 6:12)

Here are a few key points from the passage.

There is a Struggle

The Scriptures tell us there are entities called rulers, powers, world forces of darkness and spiritual forces of wickedness in heavenly places.

To grasp the reality of spiritual warfare, we must embrace the truth that there's more to this world than what we see with our natural eyes. There is a spiritual realm that is very active. Ask yourself,

"What happened to the angels that were cast out of heaven?" (Revelation 12:9)

"What has Satan been doing since he was cast out of heaven?" (Luke 10:18)

To successfully fight against these forces requires different weapons. That's why it's called "spiritual warfare."

At the point, I have a prayer for you:

"Jesus, thank you for my wild friends who have diligently read **How to Make Your Business Your Ministry**. I thank you for the call on their lives. I thank you for their desire to serve you in greater ways. I thank you for the divine connection that we have through the pages of this book. I ask that you give my friends clarity on the direction that you desire for their business and ministry. I ask that you protect them from the enemy's schemes. Let clarity rest in their mind and peace resonate in their heart. I ask that you fill every reader with joy, excitement and the boldness to finish the work to which you are calling them. Disconnect my friends from anything that seeks to kill, steal and destroy them. Instead, connect them to your faithful Word, Your plan for their life and an inspiring personal relationship with You. Amen"

The Full Armor

As I am finishing this book, so many interruptions are happening. Distractive thoughts, physical problems and fatigue are affecting me. I have friends going through challenges; I am getting offers to go out and have fun and requests to take part in worth-while events. None of these offers are wrong but when I consider the timing and the unusual number of offers that I am getting, I know it's not just a coincidence. It's easy to dismiss circumstances as mere coincidence. But inspect what's happening and ask yourself, "What was the result of the event? What was the intended goal?"

John 10:10 tells us, *"The thief comes only to steal and kill and destroy. I came that they may have life and have it abundantly."*

There is a thief who wants to steal every benefit that this book offers. He would like to destroy my witness and your belief in how God is going to use you for good. The thief doesn't care how it happens; he just wants us to stop.

The only way to wrestle this devious enemy is to follow the instructions from Scripture.

Ephesians 6:10-17 says, *"Finally, be strong in the Lord and the strength of His might. Put on the full armor of God, so that you can take your stand against the devil's schemes. For our struggle is not against flesh and blood, but against the rulers, against the authorities, against the powers of this dark world and against the spiritual forces of evil in the heavenly realms. Therefore, put on the full armor of God, so that when the day of evil comes, you may be able to stand your ground, and after you have done everything, to stand. Stand firm then, with the belt of truth buckled around your waist, with the breastplate of righteousness in place, and with your feet fitted with the readiness that comes from the gospel of peace. In addition to all this, take up the shield of faith, with which you can extinguish all the flaming arrows of the evil one. Take the helmet of salvation and the sword of the Spirit, which is the word of God."*

Are you ready to unleash your inner warrior? Are you ready to get fully dressed and take your stand? Don't worry about what you can or can't do. You have an ally in Jesus Christ, who has already won this battle.

The passage instructs us to put on the full armor. On the battlefield, the armor is for your protection. The reason we need spiritual armor is that our battle is not against flesh and blood. Our fight is with entities in the spiritual world, so our offensive and defensive weapons must be spiritual too. To put on the full armor requires a full commitment to God and His protection. The enemy looks for weakness in your armor and places where you have not fully committed to God. Remember, God already has the victory. Therefore, we boldly stand behind Him with no fear of what the enemy is trying to do. The attacks are called "schemes." That means they will not come at you in the obvious ways. The battles are subtle, tricks that often seduce you onto the wrong path.

That's why prayer is so important. Through prayer, you get clear direction from God that is supported by Scripture. Then you don't have to recognize all the devil's schemes. All you need to know is how God is leading you; everything else is counterfeit.

The beginning of your battle requires a resolve to stand. Check deep within yourself and let your inner warrior emerge. Then, decide that you will finish what you start and let nothing throw you off track.

Stand with the belt of truth

That means you are wrapping yourself with God's Word, honesty and sincerity. There is not hypocrisy operating within you. It is also called a girdle. It holds the armor together with integrity and a clear conscience.

Stand with the breastplate of righteousness

Your commitment to honor God with how you live is what carries your defensive armor. This does not mean perfection but it means that you take God's Word seriously and seek to honor Him in how you live your life. If you are in a battle but your lifestyle agrees with the enemy, it is very difficult to stand. Take a moment to reflect on your life and ask God to reveal anything that He would like to change. Ask for forgiveness and forgive others. Trust God to make you whole and new. Remember, you are not alone in the battle. The Holy Spirit helps you.

Stand with your feet fitted with the readiness that comes from the gospel

This means your mind is steadfast. You are not shuffling your feet like a person who is uncertain of their stand and the truth of the gospel. You are sure of who you are in Jesus Christ and nothing can move you off course.

Stand and take up your shield of faith

The shield referred to in this passage was large. It protected the soldier from arrows, spears and "fiery darts." Faith is your shield and your defensive weapon. It means you know you are not alone in your battles and you don't need God to explain everything before you obey. You don't have to make people understand how or why God is leading you. Use your shield and keep standing.

Stand and take your helmet of salvation

Protect your mind from attacks with the truth of salvation. One way to fortify your helmet is to know what the Bible says about your situation. Too often we enjoy a great message from an eloquent speaker. The person talking studies the Bible, then prepares a message with information they believe is important. However, when you study the Bible for yourself, you study the passage and allow God to reveal His truth directly to you in new and relevant ways. There is no substitute for studying the Bible for yourself.

Stand with the sword of the Spirit which is the Word of God

A sword is an offensive weapon. When the enemy comes at you, don't reason. Use the scripture as your weapon.

Hebrews 4:12 tells us, *"For the word of God is living and powerful, and sharper than any two-edged sword, piercing even to the division of soul and spirit, and of joints and marrow, and is a discerner of the thoughts and intents of the heart."*

Read Hebrews 4:12 slowly. God's Word is alive! It gets in you! That's why when I hear that a prominent Christian has walked away from the faith or no longer believes in salvation through Jesus Christ, I know something is seriously wrong. When God's Word is so deep within you, it pierces your bone and marrow and you can't walk away. It becomes a part of you. You hear His voice speaking to your heart; you feel His presence resting on your mind and you know He is real. It's not about understanding everything in the Bible or being perfect. It's about His life and who He is. That is where our faith rests. Trusting God and Jesus Christ's death and resurrection is the right position for a well-fought battle and the first step toward victory. Remember, it's not about you and what you can do or have done. It's about Him and what He did for us.

Positioning yourself for victory includes realizing that you have weapons available. You just need to learn how to use them. One of my favorite books of the Bible is Joshua. Caleb, Joshua and the tribes of Israel fought fearless battles in their conquest of Canaan, their promised land.

The young Israelites were born in the wilderness. They learned to trust God *before* He sent them to possess their promised land. Years earlier, Joshua and Caleb experienced a costly event that created the forty-year delay in the wilderness (Numbers 13: 17-33). This tragic event delayed their promise but eventually, the time came to finish what their parents started. Victory was theirs! Their first battle was a glorious victory against a fortified place called Jericho. Can you imagine the excitement they experienced after that battle? It was forty years before that their fathers and mothers left Egypt on what should have been a few days journey to their promised land. But after a series of decisions that went directly against God's instructions, they lost their opportunity to see the promised land and died in the wilderness. Forty years later, their children boldly finished what their parents started.

It is a hard truth to swallow but you can miss experiencing a God given promise for yourself. It doesn't mean the promise is gone because God always keeps His Word. He sometimes waits for you to follow instructions, then brings the opportunity back again when you are ready. Other times, the opportunity passes to another generation. Today, promises from God may hide in your bloodline waiting on someone to pick up the mantle and see it through. If that's you, don't let your promise wait any longer. Connect to God's plan, pick up your mantle, position yourself for victory and see it through until it is done!

After winning the great battle of Jericho, the Israelites thought the next battle against a small army would be easy. They were so sure of the victory that they decided they only needed to take a few men. They went to battle expecting a sure victory but were sent back home in defeat. What happened? How can you go from an amazing victory to an unimaginable defeat so quickly?

There was sin in the camp.

Before the battle of Jericho, God gave explicit instructions not to keep anything from Jericho for themselves (Joshua 6:17-19). But a Hebrew warrior named Achan did not follow God's instructions and took gold and silver. His decision led to Israel's defeat. That one decision interrupted the promise, led to loss of lives and halted the flow of God's divine power fighting their battle.

An interruption happened back then and it also happens today. That's why you must follow God's plan to position yourself for victory. Following God's plan and His timing requires a relationship that is so close that you understand what He tells you. You move when He says move; you wait when He says wait and you go when He says go.

"He who dwells in the shelter of the Most High will rest in the shadow of the Almighty. I will say of the Lord, He is my refuge and my fortress, my God, in whom I trust. Surely, He will save you from the fowler's snare and from the deadly pestilence. He will cover you with his feathers, and under his wings you will find refuge; his faithfulness will be your shield and rampart..." (Psalms 91:1-4)

As marketplace ministers, we have work to do. Submitting to God's plan is the only way to get the right directions to the place where you belong. God called us to this ministry and He can fully see it through. Yes, there are battles and opposing forces that also have an agenda. There's spiritual warfare to consider, hindering habits to get rid of and so many variables that make life go differently than you plan. But God's sovereignty still gets the last word.

The Lord is my light and my salvation; Whom shall I fear? The Lord is the defense of my life; Whom shall I dread? (Psalm 27:1)

How to Position Yourself for Victory

Connect with God daily

There are many best-selling books from motivational and sci-fi, to self-help and mystery but none are alive! They do not divide soul and spirit and can't judge the thoughts and intentions of the heart. These books are good for entertainment and contain great information but they can't reach into your mind and become a lamp for your feet and a light for your path (Psalm 119:105) giving you a personal infusion from God Himself!

There is a reason the Bible is the #1 best-selling book of all time. Something special happens when you study it for yourself! I don't

mean simply skimming through the pages. I mean seriously studying the Scriptures and seeking to know God, His ways and what He
wants for your life.

Conflicts occurring in our culture challenge Christians to know
God's Word. If you don't really know what you believe, anyone
can distort the truth and lead you in a direction counter to God's
Word and His will for your life. If the devil distorted scripture to
promote His own agenda (Matthew 4:1-11) with Jesus, we certainly
can expect the same to happen to us.

If you believe God's Word is true, seek to know what it says,
what it means and how to apply it to your life. Make a firm decision
on what you believe, not based on your own feelings or culture but
based on the Word of God.

When a person doesn't believe Jesus Christ is Messiah who died
for our sins, rose from the dead and is coming again, it's under-
standable why their views are based on culture, personal ideologies
and experiences. If you confess that you believe, your views and
beliefs should be based on His Word, not yours, the culture or any
other source. Of course, we are still growing but even then, God's
truth stands, even when you are still working through a process.

*"For though by this time you ought to be teachers, you have need again
for someone to teach you the elementary principles of the oracles of God,
and you have come to need milk and not solid food. For everyone who
partakes only of milk is not accustomed to the word of righteousness, for
he is an infant. But solid food is for the mature, who because of practice
have their senses trained to discern good and evil. (Hebrews 5:12-14)*

I urge you to find a Bible study that helps you learn to study
God's Word for yourself. I love great teaching and I enjoy speaking

but if I leave without giving listeners the tools they need to study for themselves, then my teaching is incomplete.

If you are a follower of Jesus Christ or want to know more about God and a relationship with Jesus Christ, make a commitment to study the Bible for yourself. It also helps to find a church, Bible study and friends who are also serious about God's Word. God will meet you right where you are. You don't have to get your life together first. You don't have to fix things. Just decide to get to know Him. When you come close to Him, things change. That's a promise! Not from me but Him (Galatians 5:22, Psalm 34:9, Psalm 1:6)!

Develop a lifestyle of prayer

The single most influential activity to position yourself for victory is prayer. We need God to keep us from falling apart. We need strength to stay in the fight. These needs require prayer for yourself and the people around you (James 5:13, Romans 12:2, Philippians 4:6).

Prayer is not just for you but also for others. They are a part of your experience; therefore, your prayer must extend to other people. Most of us spend more awake, alert hours with other people than at home with family members. You wake up early, dress for success and fight through traffic every day, just to get to work. Spending that much time in one place requires a lifestyle of prayer and prayer partners, if possible. The co-workers, even the difficult ones, need prayer. Just like a family, you can't just ignore people with whom you spend that much time. When you pray for your coworkers, you bring God's power to the workplace to override obstacles and influence the environment. You also invite God's power to create a level of success higher than you could ever accomplish on your own. Your prayer influences everyone around you.

Pray for your coworkers and for your manager. Pray for the woman in the mailroom, the security guard and the company's bottom line. When you pray for others, keep an open, non-judgmental approach. Don't be concerned about their beliefs, choices, what they do or don't do. Your job is simply to pray.

I started a prayer journal 17 years ago. I desperately needed God to move in my life in several areas. Over the years, the journal recorded many answered prayers. The prayers have changed and God has been faithful. Take some time to start your own prayer journal.

Here of some prayers to include in your journal:

- Pray for God to guide you as you approach your day.
- Pray for God to give you peace, guidance and comfort. Ask for a deeper purpose for your business and ministry.
- Pray for your family and loved ones. Bless their health, relationships, finances and family.
- Pray for God to bless your clients and affiliates. Pray for better communication and understanding.
- Ask God to protect you from false accusations and accusers.
- Pray for unity with people you work around and also pray for favor with tasks and results.
- Pray for everyone (including yourself) to function free of jealousy, pride, envy, gossip and poor attitudes.
- Pray for love, peace, and joy to rule in your business and ministry. (Galatians 5:22-23)
- Pray for God to help you and those around you with the specific issues that they face at work, at home, financially and emotionally.
- Ask God to give you profitable strategies and ideas.

Your work starts when you pray. It influences the people you work with, your clients and customers. It makes a difference to you, your family and your future. Positioning yourself for victory starts with your daily habits and prayer is the motor that makes things move the right way.

When I talk to people about problems, we pray. I pray for you, my wild friends, who share this journey with me. When I pray, I ask God to guide me, tell me what to say, give me insight. I pray for no delays and wisdom to know who to work with. I ask God to help me be a positive influence as I help people. When I review my calendar, I ask God to guide me and bless my day as well as the people that I plan to meet. Then I ask God to help me stay focused on what matters most. At the end of the week, I look back and wonder how I got it all done. Then I remember; I didn't do it alone.

You may recall me saying, "Anytime you decide to do the right thing, the wrong thing will make you an offer." There's something about trying to do what's right that attracts alternative offers. That's another reason to pray for your marketplace ministry. Most detours have a lure that romances you into a foolish decision. Prayer helps you wake up, see the detour, and get out of there! I will go a step further and say that it is doubtful that you will accomplish major, *meaningful* business and ministry milestones without developing a lifestyle of prayer.

Of course, there are many financially successful businesspeople who don't value prayer. But that's not the success we seek. We want the success that changes lives and leaves a legacy.

Now, that's worth praying for!

Self-correct quickly

I have been serving in business and ministry for well over 20 years but I still have old habits that get in the way. Every day, I must inspect myself and evaluate how I am doing. I don't expect to be perfect. Instead, I look for reasons to correct my behavior and restore my routine. Growth is a process that keeps moving, so that you never arrive. You just keep advancing to additional levels. The good news is that God helps you fulfill what He is calling you to do. Yes, He has a personal interest in your success. If you will see your weaknesses and self-correct quickly, you will land in the bullseye of your goals. It takes time but the key is to inspect, restore, and keep moving forward.

Inspect yourself

Think about the story of Achan taking the silver and gold and causing the Israelites to lose the battle at Ai. What would have happened if Achan inspected himself and realized that He made a terrible decision? Instead, he tried to hide his sin. Most times, people have time to inspect their decisions and behavior. There is often a window of opportunity to ask for forgiveness, change the action and turn around. When you inspect yourself quickly, you can make corrections in private. However, many times, when you ignore God's graceful opportunity to change your behavior, you give the enemy a gateway into your life, allowing him to tear things apart publicly.

Inspect yourself regularly and move away from issues that leave open doors for sin. Don't stand so close to the line of transgression that one thoughtless trip casts you into a battle and perhaps a consequence. Guard your reputation. Guard your marketplace ministry carefully without taking unnecessary risks.

"In all these things, we are more than conquerors through Him who loved us." (Romans 8:37)

Pray for your marketplace ministry and about your finances. A lack of funds is a hindrance in business and ministry.

Anything that has a major effect on your ministry needs constant prayer. If you are functioning as a for-profit ministry, pray about your earnings. If you are a non-profit ministry, pray for your donors, fundraising efforts and favor for new donors.

Ask God to give you creative, biblical ways to make money for your personal and ministry expenses. Ideas like creating products to offer for a price and professional services and consulting are great ways to make money for your ministry. Look for multiple streams of income to protect your business and ministry from unexpected events.

People love to comment about my multiple streams of income. Well-meaning friends often tell me, "You do too much." The answer is, my capacity is full and I love it. Of course, this level of activity is not for everyone. However, in this season of life, it's the only way to fill my cup to the brim and satisfy every beat of my heart. I haven't just filled 50% of my capacity, I'm operating at 100% and I love every moment of what I do and so can you!

Be courageous

I wish I could shield my wild friends from the battles that we face, unfortunately I can't. Even when you do all that you know to serve God, the enemy will still come for you. His intention is to stop you from accomplishing what you are about to accomplish. He wants to tear you away from a close relationship with Jesus Christ and His plan for your life and he will do anything to accomplish his goal. Thanks to God that we don't have to spend our time worrying about the enemy's threats. God has already won that victory. All we must do is walk through it and finish what we started.

"Even though I walk through the valley of the shadow of death I fear no evil, for You are with me; Your rod and Your staff, they comfort

me. You prepare a table before me in the presence of my enemies; You have anointed my head with oil; My cup overflows."(Psalm 23: 4-5)

Learn to use your weapons

I saved this section for the end of the book because it leads you to the next step and many possibilities beyond what's written in this book.

Did you know that you already have spiritual weapons? Yes, God did not send you out to build and grow a marketplace ministry while being hit by every arrow that the enemy shoots your way. Yes, we have an enemy in the spiritual realm but we also have powerful weapons that work in that realm.

After the death of a dear friend, I became a follower of Christ in college. I needed to know why I was here. I felt something in the world was bigger than me but could not figure out what it was. One day, I was walking to class feeling overwhelmed by life. A young lady was on campus, passing out little booklets about forgiveness, salvation and the love of Jesus Christ. The moment was right for me. I read it and surrendered my heart to Jesus Christ. My salvation experience was so profound that it felt like someone was gripping me and suddenly let go. It was the most peaceful moment I had ever experienced.

As time passed, I grew spiritually with an exceptional group of friends and mentors at a Bible teaching church. I started reading the Bible and running into verses like this:

"For though we walk in the flesh, we do not war according to the flesh, for the weapons of our warfare are not of the flesh, but divinely powerful for the destruction of fortresses." (2 Corinthians 10:3-4)

I kept wondering, "What are the weapons of our warfare? How many do I have and how do I use them?" That is the quest that takes you far beyond this book.

You may wonder why you need weapons for marketplace ministry. Making your business your ministry places you in an elite group of Christ followers who are effective in many areas. You are not just waiting for people to come to you. Instead, you are allowing your life to be an example in the marketplace, right where people are. Your life will tell your story and draw people to Christ and His plan for their life. It will also draw adversaries to stop you; but no worries. Our God is greater than anything or anyone who comes against you.

To get started, here are some weapons to learn to use. As you complete this book read, and meditate on the Scripture passages about one weapon each day. Make notes about interesting points and write down your questions.

Here is a list of your mighty weapons:

The Word of God

"For the word of God is living and active and sharper than any two-edged sword, and piercing as far as the division of soul and spirit, of both joints and marrow, and able to judge the thoughts and intentions of the heart." (Hebrews 4:12)

The Holy Spirit

"But to each one is given the manifestation of the Spirit for the common good. For to one is given the word of wisdom through the Spirit, and to another the word of knowledge according to the same Spirit; to another faith by the same Spirit, and to another gifts of healing by the one Spirit, and to another the effecting of miracles, and to another prophecy, and to another the distinguishing of spirits, to another various kinds of tongues, and to another the interpretation of tongues. But one and the same Spirit works all these things, distributing to each one individually just as He wills." (1 Corinthians 12:7-11)

Prayer and Fasting

"Do not be anxious about anything, but in every situation, by prayer and petition, with thanksgiving, present your requests to God. And the peace of God, which transcends all understanding, will guard your hearts and your minds in Christ Jesus. (Philippians 4:6-7)

"Is this not the fast that I have chosen: To loose the bonds of wickedness, To undo the heavy burdens, To let the oppressed go free, And that you break every yoke? (Isaiah 58:6)

"However, this kind does not go out except by prayer and fasting." (Matthew 17:21)

Praise and Worship

"But about midnight Paul and Silas were praying and singing hymns of praise to God, and the prisoners were listening to them; and suddenly there came a great earthquake, so that the foundations of the prison house were shaken; and immediately all the doors were opened, and everyone's chains were unfastened." (Acts 16:25-16)

"I will give thanks to the Lord with all my heart; I will tell of all Your wonders. I will be glad and exult in You; I will sing praise to Your name, O Most High. When my enemies turn back, they stumble and perish before You. For You have maintained my just cause;

You have sat on the throne judging righteously. You have rebuked the nations, You have destroyed the wicked; You have blotted out their name forever and ever. The enemy has come to an end in perpetual ruins." (Psalm 9:1-6)

The Name of Jesus

"For this reason also, God highly exalted Him, and bestowed on Him the name which is above every name, so that at the name of Jesus every knee will bow, of those who are in heaven and on earth and under the earth, and that every tongue will confess that Jesus Christ is Lord, to the glory of God the Father." (Philippians 2:9-11

The Blood of Christ

"John to the seven churches that are in Asia: Grace to you and peace, from Him who is and who was and who is to come, and from the seven Spirits who are before His throne, and from Jesus Christ, the faithful witness, the firstborn of the dead, and the ruler of the kings of the earth. To Him who loves us and released us from our sins by His blood and He has made us to be a kingdom, priests to His God and Father to Him be the glory and the dominion forever and ever. Amen." (Revelation 1:4-6)

Your Words and Your Testimony

"But what does it say? "The Word is near you, in your mouth and in your heart, that is, the word of faith which we are preaching, that if you confess with your mouth Jesus as Lord, and believe in your heart that God raised Him from the dead, you will be saved; for with the heart a person believes, resulting in righteousness, and with the mouth he confesses, resulting in salvation." (Romans 10:8-10)

"It is not what enters into the mouth that defiles the man, but what proceeds out of the mouth, this defiles the man." (Matthew 14:11)

"For, the one who desires life, to love and see good days, must keep his tongue from evil and his lips from speaking deceit." (1 Peter 3:10)

"Death and life are in the power of the tongue, and those who love it will eat its fruit." (Proverbs 18:21)

Angelic Help

"Are they not all ministering spirits, sent out to render service for the sake of those who will inherit salvation?" (Hebrews 1:14)

Ready for the next step? Go to MinistryinBusiness.com and read the helpful articles to jumpstart your goals.

Most of all, be encouraged. No matter where you are now, God is with you. He will guide you and take you further than you imagine. Welcome to the journey my wild friends! Let's go get our treasure.

"The Lord bless you and keep you; the Lord make his face to shine upon you and be gracious to you; the Lord lift up his countenance upon you and give you peace." (Numbers 6:24-26)

Reflections for my Wild Friends

The end of this book marks a beginning. Making your business your ministry is not something you simply learn and do. It's something you discover, experience and pursue. As the culture changes, so will you; but your foundational biblical principles will always be the same.

Fight your battle bravely, not with a deadline for God to bless you but with a commitment to stay and finish the battle.

Stay connected to other wild friends and keep God's Word in your heart. Then let the warrior that God created flow. God made you for this, my wild friend.

Bible Verses for Business Owners

"Know the Word. Live the Word."

I selected these Bible passages to encourage you in your career, business and ministry. As you apply biblical strategies to everyday work, use these passages to make decisions, deal with people and honor God. Open your heart and let God fill your void spaces. His has a plan for you to enjoy your career, even with challenges. This is how you find fulfillment. This is how you love what you do.

Philippians 1:5

"Being confident of this, that He who began a good work in you will carry it on to completion until the day of Christ Jesus."

Application: God always finishes what He starts. If He started something in you, He is not done, even if you can't see what He is doing. God's work continues until your last breath.

Colossians 3:23

"And whatever you do, do it heartily, as to the Lord and not to men."

Application: Sometimes pursuing a career feels separate from your spiritual life. Anyone can go to work on time and do their job. But it takes God's help to possess an innate attraction that draws people through you and to Him. This attraction allows you to influence people in a positive, unselfish way. As a follower of Christ, you work for Him and He promotes you. People think they are in charge, but when you are on the scene with your God-fearing work, God is the CEO who alters situations as He pleases. Work for Him and allow His timing to work things out.

If you like your job, do it well. If you don't like your job, still do it well. In both cases, God moves you forward and He needs your absolute best at the forefront.

Joshua 1:8-9

"This Book of the Law shall not depart from your mouth, but you shall meditate in it day and night, that you may observe to do according to all that is written in it. For then you will make your way prosperous, and then you will have good success. Have I not commanded you? Be strong and of good courage; do not be afraid, nor be dismayed, for the Lord your God is with you wherever you go."

Application: This verse details God's message to Joshua as he prepared to lead the Israelites on the conquest of Canaan. After forty years in the wilderness, led by Moses, a new generation and their new leader (Joshua) stood ready to fight and possess their land.

God led the Israelites into a battle that required faith for every step. They trusted God and followed the instructions in Joshua 1:8, giving them a clear path to stay focused and secure their victory.

Their strategy for success still applies to you! In the same way, as you embark on your business and faith journey, follow Joshua's lead.

- Trust God's Word
- Keep it on your mind day and night
- Do what it says
- Be strong and courageous

2 Timothy 1:7

"For God has not given us a spirit of fear, but of power and of love and of a sound mind."

Application: God wants you to stir up your spiritual gifts (2 Timothy:1:6) boldly and confidently. Use the scriptures to help you move past your fear and live in your power, love and sound mind.

James 1: 2-5

"My brethren, count it all joy when you fall into various trials, knowing that the testing of your faith produces patience. But let patience have its perfect work, that you may be perfect and complete, lacking nothing. If any of you lacks wisdom, let him ask of God, who gives to all liberally and without reproach, and it will be given to him."

Application: Trials are not always bad. Trials help you develop patience. Patience honors God and helps you focus on what is important instead of getting caught in detours. When you need help, pray about it and expect an answer, even if the answer is no or wait.

Ephesians 1: 18-19

"I ask that the eyes of your heart may be enlightened, so that you may know the hope of His calling, the riches of His glorious inheritance in the saints, and the surpassing greatness of His power to us who believe."

Application: Speak this prayer over yourself and others. Successfully moving forward requires clarity. This prayer asks God to give you what you need.

While these Bible passages keep you encouraged, this barely scrapes the surface of what God has available for you. It is through the Scriptures and an authentic relationship with Jesus Christ that you gain a fresh vision. He gives you the roadmap to accomplish your God-given goals. In marketplace ministry, knowing the Word is your foundation for effective strategies. Start here, but don't stop here. Find a Bible-based Bible study with a loving group that you trust. Find the resources offered at MinistryinBusiness.com and stay connected by joining.

Rhonda Ware Williams is a women's emPOWERment coach, educator and founder of Ministry in Business. After years of switching between a corporate career and ministry, Rhonda realized her true fulfillment was to do both. She now inspires people through writing, speaking and coaching, helping them find their personal fulfillment bullseye.

She promotes satisfaction at work without compromising your commitment to God. She has a Master of Arts degree in Christian Education with a focus on leadership. Rhonda loves helping women find freedom and priceless life applications though the scriptures.

She cherishes her marriage and quality time with her family. Her personal motto: "Each new day brings another opportunity to get it right."

Get updates and partner with Rhonda at MinistryinBusiness.com.
Follow Rhonda on X, Instagram or Linkedin @rhondawwilliams.
YouTube @RhondaWareWilliams

www.ingramcontent.com/pod-product-compliance
Lightning Source LLC
Chambersburg PA
CBHW070712130626
46553CB00005B/1959